Shakespeare's
The Comedy of Errors

Shakespeare's
The Comedy of Errors
A Psycho-Semiotic Analysis

Arthur Asa Berger

ANTHEM PRESS

Anthem Press
An imprint of Wimbledon Publishing Company
www.anthempress.com

This edition first published in UK and USA 2022
by ANTHEM PRESS
75–76 Blackfriars Road, London SE1 8HA, UK
or PO Box 9779, London SW19 7ZG, UK
and
244 Madison Ave #116, New York, NY 10016, USA

Copyright © Arthur Asa Berger 2022

The author asserts the moral right to be identified as the author of this work.

All rights reserved. Without limiting the rights under copyright reserved above, no part of this publication may be reproduced, stored or introduced into a retrieval system, or transmitted, in any form or by any means (electronic, mechanical, photocopying, recording or otherwise), without the prior written permission of both the copyright owner and the above publisher of this book.

British Library Cataloguing-in-Publication Data
A catalogue record for this book is available from the British Library.

Library of Congress Control Number: 2022933614

ISBN-13: 978-1-83998-498-3 (Pbk)
ISBN-10: 1-83998-498-8 (Pbk)

Cover image: Arthur Asa Berger drawing of Shakespeare

This title is also available as an e-book.

CONTENTS

Dedication   vii

Epigraph   viii

1   Introduction   1
    How Did I Get Here?   1
    My Books on Humor   1
    Takeaways   3

2   Theories of Humor   5
    Why We Laugh   5
    Aristotle and Superiority Theories of Comedy   6
    Incongruity and Humor   7
    Psychoanalytic (Release) Theories of Humor   8
    Humor and Paradox   9
    Disposition Theory   10
    Benign Violation Theory   11

3   Semiotics and Humor   15
    An Overview of Semiotics   15
    Metaphor   17
    Metonymy   19
    Language and Speech   19
    Codes   20

	Humor and Code Violations	22
	Syntagmatic Analysis of Texts	23
	Propp's 31 Functions of Characters	26
	Paradigmatic Analysis of Texts	26
4	Glossary: The 45 Techniques of Humor	29
	The 45 Techniques of Humor	29
	Basic Techniques of Humor Generation and Style	59
	A Note on Personality Types in Comedies	61
5	The Comedy of Errors	65
	The Persons of the Play	65
	Synopsis of *The Comedy of Errors*	65
	What is Comedy?	68
	On the Psychoanalytic Significance of Doubles	69
	On Comedic Violence	72
	The Madness Scene	77
	The Resolution of *The Comedy of Errors*	80
	Basic Humorous Techniques in *The Comedy of Errors*	83
	A Paradigmatic Analysis of *The Comedy of Errors*	85
	A Syntagmatic Analysis of *The Comedy of Errors*	86
6	Coda	89
	The Importance of Twins	89
	Semiotics and Comedy	89

References	91
About the Author	93
Index	95

This book is dedicated to my professors in the English department at the University of Massachusetts in Amherst, who inspired a love of literature in me and an appreciation of literary criticism.

Twinning Reaction: A number of psychoanalytic observers and clinicians [...] have noted that children born as twins have a tendency to (1) polarize identity characteristics in order to buttress their own selves, and (2) blur the boundaries between them and feel incomplete upon being separated from each other. Such "twinning reaction" is, however, not restricted to biological twins and can, at times, be seen in siblings born less than two years apart, or even in individuals who are not siblings but have otherwise remained close over long periods of time (e.g., marital partners).

Salman Akhtar

Central to the workings of humour in comedy is the fact that the fictional discourse of films operates on two levels of communication: the inter-character level, representing the fictional participants' interactions, and the *recipient*'s (i.e. the viewer's) level, which concerns the viewer's interpretation of the former, as carefully devised by the film production crew dubbed the *collective sender* (see Dynel 2011b and the references therein). A mass-mediated artefact, therefore, displays two layers: the characters' fictional layer, by which recipients are enthralled, and the collective sender's layer responsible for the construction of the former.

Although numerous points of similarity can be found between real-life discourse and fictional discourse (see Dynel 2011c and references therein), the two display inherent divergences. This is relevant also to the nature of humour, whose manifestations may mirror those found in real conversations or may be typical solely of film discourse, which is orientated towards *entertaining*, yet not necessarily *amusing*, the recipient (Dynel 2011a). Entertainment is here seen as being a notion superordinate to amusement. Both concern viewers' diversion and inducing their pleasurable experience, yet only the latter promotes humorous effects. Cinematic ploys and careful construction of characters' interactions facilitate the occurrence of various humour forms sometimes based on communicative phenomena which would either be impossible in everyday discourse or, if materialised, would not carry any humorousness for any participant.

Marta Dynel, "Humorous Phenomena in Dramatic Discourse"
European Journal of Humour Research **1(1) 22–60**

Chapter 1

INTRODUCTION

How Did I Get Here?

In writing this book I had to ask myself, "how does a person who wrote his Ph.D. dissertation on Al Capp's comic strip, *Li'l Abner*, and spent fifty years writing about pop culture, end up writing a book on one of Shakespeare's comedies?" The answer is that *Li'l Abner* was a humorous comic strip, and my dissertation, published in 1970 as *Li'l Abner: A Study in American Satire*, showed my early interest in the scholarly study of humor.

Figure 1.1 William Shakespeare.

My Books on Humor

I have been writing about humor since 1970 and have written about humor in many articles and about humorous comic strips in my book, *The Comic-Stripped American* (1974) and humorous television shows in my book, *The TV-Guided American* (1975). I've also written about Jewish humor in my books *The Genius of the Jewish Joke* (Jason Aronson, 1997) and *Jewish Jesters: A Study in American Popular Comedy* (2001, Hampton Press). I've written about humor, in general, in four books: *An Anatomy of Humor, The Art of Comedy Writing, Blind Men and Elephants: Perspectives on Humor* and *Humor Psyche and Society.*

An Anatomy of Humor was published in 1993 by Transaction Books and features what I describe as a "Glossary" of the 45 techniques of humor that I discovered in researching humor. The book also has chapters on jokes, Mickey Mouse, *Huckleberry Finn, Twelfth Night* and Jewish fools. I will say more about these 45 techniques later and offer a revised version of my glossary, since the techniques are central to my analysis of humorous texts. It has many jokes in the book that I analyze and I provide a list of humorous jokes and texts in a separate index in the book.

My next book, *Blind Men and Elephants: Perspectives on Humor* (Transaction, 1995), has chapters on different disciplinary approaches to the subject: communications, sociological, semiotic, psychological and so on. It also has many jokes in the book and a separate index of jokes. My third book with Transaction (1997), *The Art of Comedy Writing*, deals with theatrical comedies and has a long chapter on the 45 techniques of humor which it then applies to a play by Plautus, *Miles Gloriosus*, Shakespeare's *Twelfth Night*, Sheridan's *The School of Scandal* (1777) and Ionesco's remarkable "theater of the absurd" play, *The Bald Soprano*. It is an analysis of elite culture texts and, as such, serves as a precursor to my book on Shakespeare.

I also see myself as a humorist and have written some academic murder mysteries that are comedic in nature. In one of my mysteries, *Postmortem for a Postmodernist* (1997, AltaMira Press), I kill my victim, Ettore Gnocchi (potato dumpling), on the first page in four different ways. His wife was named Shoshana TelAviv. My detective in this novel is named Solomon (wisdom) Hunter. Many of my mysteries have Sherlock Holmes as the detective.

My book, *The Jewish Jesters*, has chapters on Groucho Marx, Jack Benny, Henny Youngman, Rodney Dangerfield, Sid Caesar, Lenny Bruce, Mel Brooks, Jackie Mason, Woody Allen and Jerry Seinfeld—the most important Jewish comedians of recent, and not so recent, years. It also contains many jokes and humorous texts, since I believe that books about humor should also have lots of humor in them. So I've been writing about humor for many years and have a set of comedy techniques I can use in analyzing humor that I can apply to Shakespeare's works. I also am a semiotician and that will play an important role in this book. I would consider my 45 techniques and my discussion of syntagmatic and paradigmatic analysis as semiotic in nature and I will offer a discussion of semiotic theories and concepts in this book for readers not familiar with the subject.

Takeaways

When you read this book, you will learn about:

Different theories of humor that deal with why we laugh: superiority theory, incongruity theory, release/psychoanalytic theory and cognitive theory.

My typology of the 45 techniques of humor, which, I argue, is found in all forms of humor and humorous texts from Roman times to the present. Writers of comedies have learned these techniques over the course of their careers but, I believe, generally are not conscious of them.

The techniques of humor that Shakespeare used so brilliantly in *The Comedy of Errors* and his other comedies. I point out in my analysis of *The Comedy of Errors* many places where Shakespeare has used one or another technique.

Semiotic theory, including concepts such as signifiers and signifieds, codes, metaphor and metonymy and their importance in analyzing humorous texts.

Psychoanalytic theories about twins.

Psychoanalytic theories about comedy and humor.

How to make a paradigmatic (from the work of Lévi-Strauss) and syntagmatic (from Vladimir Propp's *Morphology of the Folktale*) analysis of a humorous text. This book teaches you how to analyze humorous texts and offers, as an example, my discussion of *The Comedy of Errors*.

Ideas on the nature of humor, comedy, jokes and Shakespeare's comedy from important scholars in many academic disciplines.

A joke is a play upon form. It brings into relation disparate elements in such a way that one accepted pattern is challenged by the appearance of another which in some way was hidden in the first. I confess that I find Freud's definition of the joke highly satisfactory. The joke is an image of the relaxation of conscious control in favor of the subconscious [...] The joke merely affords opportunity for realizing that an accepted pattern has no necessity. Its excitement lies in the suggestion that any particular ordering of experience may be arbitrary and subjective. It is frivolous in that it produces no real alternative, only an exhilarating sense of freedom from form in general. [...]

My hypothesis is that a joke is seen and allowed when it offers a symbolic pattern of a social pattern occurring at the same time. As I see it, all jokes are expressive of the social situations in which they occur. The one social condition necessary for a joke to be enjoyed is that the social group in which it is received should develop the formal characteristics of a "told" joke: that is, a dominant pattern of relations is challenged by another. If there is no joke in the social structure, no other joking can occur.

Mary Douglas. "Jokes" in Mary Douglas, *Implicit Meanings: Essays in Anthropology*. London: Routledge and Kegan Paul. 1975: 96, 98.

Chapter 2

THEORIES OF HUMOR

I distinguish between *why* people laugh and *what makes people laugh*. They are different matters. Nobody knows why we laugh, though over the millennia, philosophers, psychologists, sages and theorists of one kind or another have tried to answer this question. Aristotle suggested, for example, that we laugh at people made ridiculous, which suggests that *superiority* is the reason why we laugh. Other philosophers have suggested that *incongruity* is the basis of all humor; we expect something and get something else. You find this in the punch lines of jokes. Freud and many psychoanalytically inclined scholars suggest that *masked aggression* is the basis of humor. Gregory Bateson and others like him have argued that humor involves cognition and various forms of *processing communication* and meta-communications to generate humor. There are endless theories on why people laugh, but no general agreement on the matter, though I would say that incongruity theories tend to be dominant.

Why We Laugh

Humor is a subject that has attracted the attention and interest of some of our greatest minds, from Aristotle and Kant to Bergson and Freud. Humor has fascinated psychologists, sociologists, philosophers, linguists and many other kinds of scholars and thinkers. It has also fascinated and played an important part in the work of our greatest writers, such as Cervantes, Shakespeare, Moliere, Swift and Twain. One could cite many others. Yet, curiously, after thousands of years spent trying to understand humor, there is still a great deal of controversy about what humor is, what humor does, and why something is funny. On Google, under "Humor Theory," we find 19,500,000 results and on Amazon.com books we find over 10,000 books. (Accessed 10/20/2021).

There are, however, some important theories on this matter which I would like to discuss here. I will start with superiority theories.

Figure 2.1 Aristotle.

Aristotle and Superiority Theories of Comedy

For Aristotle, comedy (and I will use the terms humor and comedy interchangeably, though comedy is, technically speaking, a literary form) is based on "an imitation of men worse than the average," of people who are "ridiculous." Hobbes, in a classic formulation, carried the same idea a bit further. As he put it in *The Leviathan* (Part I, Chapter 6):

> Sudden glory, is the passion which makes those grimaces called laughter; and is caused either by some sudden act of their own, that pleases them; or by the apprehension of some deformed thing in another, by comparison whereof they suddenly applaud themselves. And it is incident most to them, that are conscious of the fewest abilities in themselves; who are forced to keep themselves in their own favor by observing the imperfections of other men. And therefore much laughter at the defects of others, is a sign of pusillanimity. For of great minds, one of the proper works is, to help and free others from scorn; and to compare themselves only with the most able.

Hobbes was primarily a political philosopher and, at first sight, it might seem strange for the author of a book on political philosophy to write about humor.

We now recognize that there is a relationship between humor and power, perhaps the key concept in political thought, and this relationship has attracted a considerable amount of attention, especially in recent years. That is because we now can see that humor can be a subtle and powerful means of social control by the dominant elements in society. And it is, at the same time, a force for resistance by the subordinate elements in society. It is only natural, then, that Hobbes, being a philosopher of power, was interested in humor and its utility for those in power. (The relationship between humor and power is the subject of a book, *Humor, and Society: Resistance and Control*, which was edited by two British scholars, Chris Powell and George E. Paton.) Their subtitle suggests the "double-edged" sword aspect of humor: It can be used as a means of resistance to power and it can be used, by the powerful, to control people.

Incongruity and Humor

There is another theory that is probably the most important and most widely accepted of the explanations of humor. This is the incongruity theory of humor, which argues that all humor involves some kind of difference between what one expects and what one gets. The term "incongruity" has many meanings—inconsistent, not harmonious, lacking propriety and not conforming, so there are many possibilities hidden in the term. Incongruity theories involve the intellect, though they may not seem to at first sight, for we have to recognize an incongruity before we can laugh at one (though this recognition process takes place very quickly and is probably done subconsciously). Incongruity theorists often argue that superiority theories are really special forms of incongruity.

Immanuel Kant can be considered an incongruity theorist. He argued that humor doesn't yield the experience of beauty, but that of pleasure. Beauty is something profound and long-lasting, while pleasure is superficial and momentary. He wrote, "Laughter is an affection arising from the sudden transformation of a strained expectation into nothing" (quoted in Piddington, 1963: 28).

Arthur Schopenhauer offers another description of incongruity theory:

> Many human actions can only be performed by the help of reason and deliberation, and yet there are some which are better performed without its assistance. This very incongruity of sensuous and abstract knowledge, on account of which the latter always merely approximates to the former, as mosaic approximates to painting, is the cause of a very remarkable phenomenon which, like reason itself, is peculiar to human nature, and of which the explanations that have ever anew been attempted, as insufficient: I mean laughter. [...] The cause of laughter in

every case is simply the sudden perception of the incongruity between a concept and the real objects which have been thought through it in some relation, and laughter itself is just the expression of this incongruity. (1818/1844 [1907], Book I, sec. 13)

So there is an incongruity between what we might expect and what we get, which helps us understand how punch lines in jokes work.

Psychoanalytic (Release) Theories of Humor

One of the more interesting and controversial theories of humor stems from the work of Freud. The psychoanalytic theory of humor argues that humor is essentially masked aggression (often of a sexual nature) which gives us gratifications we desperately crave. As Freud wrote in his classic book, *Jokes and Their Relation to the Unconscious*,

> And here at last we can understand what it is that jokes achieve in the service of their purpose. They make possible the satisfaction of an instinct (whether lustful or hostile) in the face of an obstacle that stands in its way.

With smutty jokes, Freud tells us, we get pleasure because women will not tolerate "undisguised sexuality," so we mask our sexual aggressiveness by

Figure 2.2 Sigmund Freud.

humor. We also derive pleasure camouflaging our aggression and hostility (and thus evading the strictures of our super-egos) or regressing to child-like stages, among other things. Freud's analysis of humor devotes a good deal of attention to the formal or structural properties of jokes. It is not only their subjects that are important but also the forms and the techniques they employ, such as wordplay, condensation and displacement. Freud's writing on techniques led me to conduct my research and my "discovery" of the various techniques of humor.

He also recounts many wonderful Jewish jokes in the book and alludes to the remarkable amount of self-criticism found in jokes that Jews tell about themselves. "Incidentally," he wrote, "I do not know whether there are many other instances of a people making fun to such a degree of its own character." His use of the word "fun" is important. He did not regard Jewish jokes as masochistic. Just the opposite. Jews are not the only ones to make fun of themselves, I might point out. And there are good reasons for this kind of behavior.

This "fun" that the Jews make of their character is connected to their social marginality and is an effective means of countering and dealing with the difficulties they have faced in trying to live in societies that have frequently been very hostile. It might be argued that since humor is an effective way of keeping in touch with reality, Jewish humor has been intimately connected with Jewish survival. There is, we can see here, an important social dimension of humor. It is not some kind of trivial matter, but enables people to gain valuable insights into social and political matters.

Humor and Paradox

There is another theory of humor to consider, and that might be described as a conceptual theory. It argues that humor is best understood as dealing with communication, paradox, play and the resolution of logical problems. This, at least, is the argument of many cognitive theorists (though Freud also concerned himself with cognitive jokes, which suggests that he had cognition covered, to some degree, in his psychoanalytic theory of humor).

William Fry, a psychiatrist who worked with Gregory Bateson at one time, has explained how paradox is related to humor. He writes, in *Sweet Madness* (1968:153):

> During the unfolding of humor, one is suddenly confronted by an explicit-implicit reversal when the punch line is delivered. The reversal helps distinguish humor from play, dreams, etc. [...] But the reversal also has the unique effect of forcing upon the humor participants

an internal redefining of reality. Inescapably, the punch line combines communication and meta-communication.

Thus, at one stroke, the punch line in jokes gives us information which, if the joke is good, tells us about the world, strikes us as funny and functions as meta-communication (that tells us that what we have heard is "unreal").

Gregory Bateson offers more insights into the paradoxical theory of humor in "The Position of Humor in Human Communication" (Macy Conferences 1952).

> Of the three types of convulsion, laughter is the one for which there is the clearest ideational content. It is relatively easy to discuss what is a joke, what are the characteristics that make a joke, what is the point of a joke. The sort of analysis that I want to propose assumes that the messages in the first phase of telling the joke are such that while the informational content is, so to speak, on the surface, the other content types in various forms are implicit in the background. When the point of a joke is reached, suddenly this background material is brought into attention and a paradox, or something like it is touched off. A circuit of contradictory notions is completed. [...] These paradoxes arise when a message about the message is contained in the message. [...] The hypothesis that I am presenting is that the paradoxes are the prototypic paradigm for humor, and that laughter occurs at the moment when a circuit of that kind is completed. This hypothesis could be followed up with an analysis of jokes, but rather than do that, I should like to present to you the notion that these paradoxes are the stuff of human communication.
>
> *https://www.coursehero.com/file/75061754/Bateson-1952-1pdf/*

For Bateson, the paradox is not only central to humor but also to human communication of all kinds.

Disposition Theory

This theory proposes (Zillmann and Cantor, 1976:100–101) that

> Humor appreciation varies inversely with the favorableness of the disposition toward the agent or the entity being disparaged, and varies directly with the favorableness of the disposition toward the agent or the entity disparaging it.

Wikipedia offers another description of the topic:

> **Affective disposition theory** (**ADT**), in its simplest form, states that media and entertainment users make moral judgments about characters in a narrative which in turn affects their enjoyment of the narrative. This theory was first posited by Zillmann and Cantor (1977), and many offshoots have followed in various areas of entertainment (Raney, 2006a). Entertainment users make constant judgments of a character's actions, and these judgments enable the user to determine which character they believe is the "good guy" or the "villain". However, in an article written in 2004, Raney examined the fundamental ADT assumption that viewers of drama always form their dispositions toward characters through moral judgment of motives and conduct. Raney argued that viewers/consumers of entertainment media could form positive dispositions toward characters before any moral scrutinizing occurs. He proposed that viewers sometimes develop story schemas that provide them "with the cognitive pegs upon which to hang their initial interpretations and expectations of characters" (Raney, 2004, p. 354). The basic idea of the affective disposition theory is used as a way to explain how emotions become part of the entertainment experience.
>
> *https://en.wikipedia.org/wiki/Affective_disposition_theory*

Benign Violation Theory

An article, "Humorous Complaining," by A. Peter McGraw, Caleb Warren and Christina Kan, offers a description of this theory:

> Although being humorous can be positive and beneficial, scholars for millennia have also recognized that negative situations and stimuli often trigger humor (Martin, 2007; McGraw and Warner 2014; Warren and McGraw 2013a). As a theoretical foundation, we draw on the benign violation theory, which suggests that the same negative, disappointing situations that trigger complaints are also a ripe source of humor. The theory proposes that humor occurs when something that is perceived to threaten a person's well-being, identity, or normative belief structure (i.e., a violation) simultaneously seems okay or acceptable (i.e., benign; McGraw and Warren 2010; McGraw, Warren, et al. 2012; Rozin et al. 2013; Veatch 1998). Developmentally, violations are likely first perceived as physical threats, such as a parent's disappearance in peek-a-boo, but later expand to include threats to identity (e.g., insult humor), logic (e.g.,

elephant jokes; absurdities), communication rules (e.g., sarcasm; puns), and social conventions (e.g., breaking a dress code).

> Journal of Consumer Research, *Vol. 41, No. 5 (February 2015), pp. 1153–1171 Published by: Oxford University Press.*

We can see from this survey of theories of humor that thinkers from Aristotle's time to the present have been interested in making sense of humor and very inventive in elaborating different perspectives and methodologies for analyzing the subject.

This chapter discusses the semiotics of humor. Semiotics considers signs of any kind, not just linguistic ones. The distinction between denotative semiotics and connotative semiotics is introduced. Humor is a connotative semiotics, and it thus shares some of the features of connotative semiotics, such as the defunctionalization of the sign (i.e., messages are no longer used to communicate, but for ulterior purposes, i.e., to amuse or for play). Bateson's theory of play is also introduced in this context. This leads to the definition of humor as a message whose perlocutionary goal is to be perceived as humorous (rather than, say, informative). Two significant conclusions are drawn: the mechanisms of humor are the same in linguistic and non-linguistic communication and the semantic and pragmatic mechanisms of humor are the determining factors of the unique features of humorous communication.

Salvatore Attardo, "Semiotics of Humor"
Published to Oxford Scholarship Online: September 2020
DOI: 10.1093/oso/9780198791270.001.0001

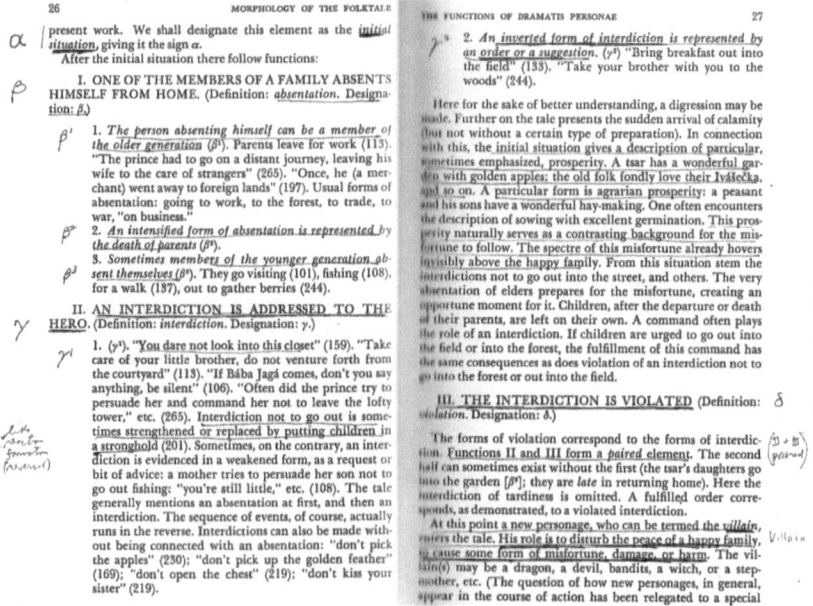

Figure 3.1 Pages from Propp's *Morphology of the Folktale*.

Chapter 3

SEMIOTICS AND HUMOR

The semiotic theory of humor is allied to the cognitive theory. Semiotics asks how meaning is generated in daily life and, for our purposes, in any text. It seeks to answer this question by analyzing the signification found in a given text and by trying to elicit the polar oppositions (or sets of paired opposites) implicit in any work. It also seeks to understand the way the narrative functions (when there is one). These two operations involve investigating the paradigmatic (or oppositional) and the syntagmatic (or linear, narrative) aspects of the text. According to the French anthropologist Claude Lévi-Strauss, the syntagmatic analysis of a text tells us the manifest content, what the text (a joke or any other form of humor) is about, and the paradigmatic analysis tells us the latent content, what the joke "really" means. And this meaning is hidden; it is not the same as the subject of the joke or work of humor or text.

An Overview of Semiotics

Since many people are not familiar with semiotics, I offer here an overview of some of its basic concepts.

Ferdinand de Saussure's book, *Course in General Linguistics*, published in 1915 (and in an English translation in 1959) is not known to the general public. And Saussure is not a name that many people are familiar with—the way they are with Freud, Darwin, Einstein or Marx. But this book is, we now recognize, a seminal book, one of the most important books published in the twentieth century, and Saussure's ideas have influenced scholars not only in linguistics but in many other disciplines.

Saussure is the founding father of semiology—which means, literally, "words about" or "the study of" (logos, logy) signs (sēmeîon). Sēmeîon is the Greek word for sign. An American philosopher, Charles Sanders Peirce, developed a different theory of signs, which he called semiotics, and it is semiotics that is now accepted as the term to be used for the study of signs.

But what's a sign? And how do signs function? For our purposes, let me define a sign as "anything that can be made to stand for something else."

Figure 3.2 Ferdinand de Saussure.

Thus, words are signs. When we use the word "tree" we are using it to stand for a large plant with leafy branches. We have to learn what the word "tree" stands for just as we have to learn what all words and most signs stand for. Facial expressions are signs. Winks are signs. Body movements (body language) are signs. So are our haircuts, the color of our hair (blue, green, orange, etc.), the style of our eyeglasses, earrings we may or may not wear, mustaches and beards, jewelry, clothes, shoes—the list goes on and on. Objects are signs; we are aware of this and sometimes use the term "status symbol." So, I would suggest, we're all dimly conscious of the fact that signs play an important role in social life. Costuming, hairstyles, body language, facial expressions and so on also are very important in theater and, for our interests, in Shakespeare's comedies.

Everything we do and everything we wear can be seen, then, as a message (generated by a sign) and we spend our lives sending messages about ourselves and interpreting messages that others send about themselves. We're not always conscious that we are sending messages, just as others aren't always conscious that they are receiving or sending messages either. So we spend a great deal of time sending messages to others and decoding—trying to make sense of—the messages others are sending us. Sometimes we don't send the message we think we are sending, and frequently others misinterpret the messages we send, which can create problems.

So signs are tricky and understanding how they function is, actually, quite complicated. The thing that makes understanding them difficult is that the relationship between the sign and the message (technically the signifier and the signified) is arbitrary, based on convention—which means that most of the time we have to learn what signs mean.

Consider, also, some signs that we are conscious of and which are part of our everyday lives: roadside billboards, traffic signs (and signals), package designs, signs in shops, sign language, baseball signs (given by catcher to pitcher) or football signs (given by coaches on the sidelines), obscene gestures, super graphics, "message" tee shirts, labels on articles of clothing, zodiac signs, our fingerprints, our signatures, bumper stickers and uniforms. It's not too much of an exaggeration to say that human beings are sign-creating and sign-interpreting animals. Many aspects of semiotics also deal with language, such as metaphor (and a weaker form of metaphor, simile) and metonymy (and a weaker form of metonymy, synecdoche) that are important for us to know

Metaphor

We seldom think about it, but much of our communication is done by making analogies (my boyfriend is a "hunk" or my love is a rose). The technical term for communicating by analogy is metaphor. When we use a metaphor we experience, we understand, or we explain one thing in terms of something else. Thus, in the examples above, we are equating two things saying:

My boyfriend *is* a hunk.
My love *is* a rose.

There is a weaker form of metaphor called simile, in which we say that something is like something else. Here, we use "like" or "and" to weaken the comparison:

My love *is like* a rose.

Many of us learn about metaphors and similes in literature classes and assume that metaphors are devices used by poets and writers, but don't play much of a role in our everyday lives. That conclusion is wrong, for metaphor plays a major role in the way we think.

As George Lakoff and Mark Johnson explain in *Metaphors We Live By* (1980:3):

Metaphor is pervasive in everyday life, not just in language but in thought and action. Our ordinary conceptual system, in terms of which we both think and act, is fundamentally metaphoric in nature. The concepts that govern our thought are not just matters of the intellect. They also govern our everyday functioning, down to the most mundane details. Our concepts structure what we perceive, how we get around in the world, and how we relate to other people. Our conceptual system thus plays a central role in defining our everyday realities. If we are right in suggesting that our conceptual system is largely metaphorical, then the way we think, what we experience, and what we do every day is very much a matter of metaphor.

Lakoff and Johnson suggest that there are many kinds of metaphors. Some of the important ones are:

Structural metaphors. They shape how we think, act and make sense of the world.

Example: Time is money.

Orientational metaphors. They deal with our orientation in space, generally in terms of polar oppositions, such as up/down, central/ peripheral and front/back.

Example: Happy is up; sad is down.

Ontological metaphors. They help us interpret life in terms of common objects and substances that we frequently personify.

Example: The mind is a machine.

Many expressions we use in our day-to-day speech are based on these three kinds of metaphors, as in (structural) "I don't have time to give you," (orientational) "I'm really feeling down" and (ontological) "I've been busy cranking out term papers."

Metaphors pervade our thinking and our speech, though we seldom pay much attention to them. And what is more important, there are logical implications for the metaphors we hold and use that we seldom are aware of, but which often play an important, though unrecognized, role in our lives.

Here's an example from the play, which uses a simile:

ANTIPHOLUS OF SYRACUSE
I to the world am like a drop of water
That in the ocean seeks another drop,
Who, falling there to find his fellow forth,
Unseen, inquisitive, confounds himself.
So I, to find a mother and a brother,

Metonymy

A great deal of the communicating we do involves analogies (metaphors and similes) but there is another means of generating meaning that is equally important, and that involves using associations. As we grow up in a society we learn all kinds of things: from our schools, stories we hear, reading books (or having books read to us), reading comics, watching television, listening to the radio, going to movies, talking with friends and so on. We become acculturated and accumulate a storehouse of information that we use to make sense of things and to function in society.

This means that each of us, in a given culture, has a great deal of commonly held information that we use to interpret messages we hear or texts we see. The technical term for this phenomenon, using associations to generate meaning, is metonymy. We transfer information we have about one thing to something else, or we use one thing to refer to something that is associated with or related to it.

As Lakoff and Johnson write in *Metaphors We Live By* (1980:36):

> Metaphor and metonymy are different *kinds* of processes. Metaphor is principally a way of conceiving of one thing in terms of another, and its primary function is understanding. Metonymy, on the other hand, has primarily a referential function, that is, allows us to use one entity to *stand for* another. But metonymy is not merely a referential device. It also serves the function of providing understanding.

One thing we must recognize is that frequently an object can function both metaphorically and metonymically at the same time. Thus, in a famous Fidji ad, the snake around the woman's neck can be seen as both a phallic symbol (metaphor) and as something that suggests (metonymy) the snake in the Garden of Eden. The text in this ad helps us recognize this association since it says that Fidji is "the perfume of paradise regained."

Language and Speech

Language, Saussure tells us, is not to be confused with speech.

Language is a social institution that defines how words are to be used and what words mean; speech, on the other hand, involves the words a particular person uses and the way those words are used. As Saussure writes in his *Course in General Linguistics* (1966:14):

> Language is a well-defined object in the heterogeneous mass of speech facts. It can be localized in the limited segment of the speaking-circuit where an auditory image becomes associated with a concept. It is the

social side of speech, outside the individual who can never create or modify it by himself; it exists only by virtue of a sort of contract signed by the members of the community. Moreover, the individual must always serve an apprenticeship in order to learn the functioning of a language; a child assimilates it only gradually.

Language and speech are interdependent, Saussure adds, but they are absolutely distinct from one another. You have to know a language in order to communicate with others, but since language is based on rules and conventions, it is affected by speech.

The most important differences found in language involve opposition. Saussure suggested that oppositions are central to language. And another great linguist, Roman Jakobson, argued that using binary oppositions is the fundamental way the human mind produces meaning. It is the nature of language that "forces" us, so to speak, to think in oppositions such as mother/father, up/down, inside/outside, rich/poor, happy/sad and so on. A useful analogy would be to think of the human mind as being like a computer (itself a binary device based on 1's and 0's) that immediately (and without our awareness of it much of the time) generates an opposition in our minds for every concept we use.

Codes

You need codes to understand what words mean and what objects signify. Daniel Chandler, a semiotician, explains the relationship between signs and codes in his book *Semiotics: The Basics* (2002:147):

> Since the meaning of a sign depends on the code within which it is situated, codes provide a framework within which signs make sense. Indeed, we cannot grant something the status of a sign if it does not function within a code....The conventions of codes represent a social dimension in semiotics: a code is a set of practices familiar to users of the medium operating with a broad cultural framework.... When studying cultural practices, semioticians treat as signs any objects or actions which have meaning to the members of a cultural group, seeking to identify the rules or conventions of the codes which underlie the production of meaning within that culture.

The signs Chandler is writing about involve gestures, foods, rituals and just about everything we say and do, what we look like, how we talk and so on. This is because objects and other kinds of signs have meaning and semiotics helps us understand how to make sense of these signs. Chandler points out that there are many kinds of codes. For example, for social codes he lists:

Verbal language
Bodily codes
Commodity codes
Fashions, clothing, cars
Behavioral codes
Protocols, rituals, role-playing, games

We have to know the codes to function in society and to understand what is going on in narratives of one kind or another and when, for example, we are to regard a narrative as humorous. It may be that humorists are code violators and it is this ability to violate codes of logic and social codes that frees them to create humor.

Saussure, one of the founding fathers of the science of signs (he called his version of it "semiology"), reminds us that signs have two parts: a sound-image or signifier and a concept or signified. The relation between the signifier and signified is arbitrary, a matter of convention, so we all have to learn what signs mean. In essence, we learn a number of codes, which can be thought of as rules that tell us how to interpret signs. Saussure called his science of signs "semiology" in contrast to C.S. Peirce, another important theorist of signs, who called his science "semiotics".

He argued that there are three kinds of signs: icons, which signify by resemblance; indexes, which signify by cause and effect; and symbols, whose meaning must be learned. The term "semiotics" is the one most commonly

Figure 3.3 C.S. Peirce.

used now for the study of signs and I will use the term for either perspective on signs.

Humor and Code Violations

From a semiotic point of view, humor can be thought of as often involving some kind of code violation. This notion can be thought of as a semiotic variation on the concept of incongruity. According to incongruity theorists, humor is based on some kind of surprise, in which what you get is not what you expect. In jokes, when you reach the punch line, there is a resolution of the story that is surprising and it is this unexpected resolution that generates the laughter. Logic would dictate that a text should end in a certain way that is tied, somehow, to the events told in the text. But in joke texts, punch lines always confound us and offer resolutions of situations (created in the joke's narrative) that are unanticipated. Jokes, let us remember, are defined as short narratives meant to amuse that have punch lines.

In an article, Jokes as text type in *Humor* (1992, vol. 5, No. 1/2), Salvatore Attardo and Jean-Charles Chabanne argue that jokes satisfy the requirements that various semioticians have elaborated to qualify as texts. They define jokes as follows: (1992, 172):

> A joke is an anonymous, partially or completely recycled text that contains a non-bonafide linguistic/cognitive disturbance (the punch line) that "closes" the previous text. The text itself is tendentially short and contains the basic features of a narrative.

Figure 3.4 Vladimir Propp.

They consider jokes to be "micro-narratives" that contain all the features of traditional narrative texts, along with the necessary punch lines.

The notion of humor as a kind of code violation is also close to Bergson's view that humor involves the mechanical that is encrusted on the living. Comedy, as has been pointed out, is often based on bizarre types—characters who are monomaniacs, fixated on one particular passion, dominated by a humor: some are misers, some are hypochondriacs, some are boasters and so on. This, we can say, represents a violation of the code that humans are supposed to be reasonable individuals, that we should be flexible and fit in with others, and not cause all kinds of complications by being so one-dimensional, so rigid.

Syntagmatic Analysis of Texts

A syntagm is a chain and so a syntagmatic analysis of a text looks at the linear or narrative structure of a text to see how the elements in the texts are linked together. A sentence is a syntagm of words and a film or television show is a syntagm of images, as well as words, sounds and music. Editing, then, is a syntagmatic activity that involves dealing with the sequential or linear progression of words, images, whatever. If you think about it, a joke is a syntagmatic narrative in which various statements follow one another until the punchline is reached and the joke is resolved, usually with some kind of a surprise. The diagram below shows this syntagmatic structure graphically.

$$A \rightarrow B \rightarrow C \rightarrow D \rightarrow E \text{ (punchline)}$$
$$\downarrow$$
$$F \text{ (mirthful laughter)}$$

Diagram of a joke

I offer a joke and its analysis below.

The Minister, The Priest and The Rabbi, and the Minister's Wife Joke.

A minister returns unexpectedly early to his house and finds the strong smell of cigar smoke and his wife naked in bed. He looks out the window and sees a priest smoking a big cigar walking out of the door of his apartment house. In a jealous rage, he picks up the refrigerator and throws it on the priest, killing him instantly. Then, smitten by remorse, he jumps out the window and kills himself. The next instant, the minister, the priest, and a rabbi appear before an angel at the Pearly Gates. "What happened?" the angel asks the priest. "I was walking out of this house and a refrigerator fell on me," said the priest. "And you?" asks the angel to the minister. "I threw the refrigerator on the priest and then felt so bad I killed myself." "And you?" ask the angel to the rabbi. "You've got me," says the rabbi. "I was minding my own business, smoking a cigar in a refrigerator...."

The joke's punch line, "I was minding my own business, smoking a cigar in a refrigerator" is meant to elicit mirthful laughter in those who hear the joke or read it. Generally, we find several different techniques in a joke, though there is usually one dominant technique. The most important technique in the joke about the minister, priest and rabbi, I would suggest, is one I call "Mistakes."

The minister sees the priest smoking a cigar and assumes he has been with his wife. He was actually correct, but his behavior is based on an unproven assumption that the cigar smoke was from the priest. There is also "Facetiousness." In this joke, we find that the rabbi has a rather latitudinarian perspective on his sexual liaison with the minister's wife. In addition, there is the "repetition," in which we are introduced to the minister, then the priest and then the rabbi.

The main techniques found in this joke (based on my typology of humorous techniques) are:

29: mistakes	cigar smoke was from a rabbi in the refrigerator, not the priest
19: facetiousness	I was minding my own business
33: exposure	minister's wife is unfaithful
34: repetition	the minister, the priest, the rabbi and the angel

These techniques are explained in considerable detail in the next chapter.

Syntagmatic Analysis

One of the earliest, most accessible, influential and useful studies of the sequential nature of narratives is Vladimir Propp's *Morphology of the Folktale,* published in 1928. Though Propp deals with folktales (his book dealt with several hundred Russian folktales), his methodology can be used to analyze all kinds of texts, such as stories, novels, television shows, plays and films.

Wherever there is a narrative, that is, a text with a linear sequential structure, Propp's method can be used. The term "morphology" comes from botany and means a study of the component parts of a plant. Propp studied the parts of narratives.

Propp looked at other means of dealing with texts, such as focusing on their plots and themes, and concluded that all the methodologies he studied were useless. They contradicted themselves or created classification systems that broke down. He argued that the best way of studying narratives was in terms of what he called their "functions," which he defined as acts of characters analyzed in terms of their significance for the course of action in the text. He claimed that there were a limited number of these functions and that they are the common elements in all the tales he studied.

Table 3.1 Propp' Functions in His Morphology of The Folktale.

	Initial situation	Members of a family are introduced
1.	Absentation	A member of the family absents himself.
2.	Interdiction	An interdiction is given to the hero.
3.	Violation	The interdiction is violated.
4.	Reconnaissance	A villain attempts to get information.
5.	Delivery	The villain gets information about the victim.
6.	Trickery	The villain tries to deceive the victim.
7.	Complicity	The victim is deceived.
8.	Villainy	The villain causes harm to a family member
8a.	Lack	A family member lacks or desires something.
9.	Mediation	A misfortune is made known and the hero is dispatched.
10.	Counteraction	The hero (seeker) agrees to counteraction.
11.	Departure	The hero leaves home.
12.	First donor function	The hero tested, receives magical agent from a donor.
13.	Hero's reaction	The hero reacts to an agent or donor.
14.	Receipt of agent	The hero acquires the use of a magical agent.
15.	Spatial change	The hero is led to the object of his search.
16.	Struggle	The hero and the villain join in combat.
17.	Branding	The hero is branded.
18.	Victory	The hero defeats the villain.
19.	Liquidation	Initial misfortune or lack is liquidated.
20.	Return	The hero returns.
21.	Pursuit, chase	The hero is pursued.
22.	Rescue	The hero is rescued from pursuit.
23.	Unrecognized arrival	The hero, unrecognized, arrives home or elsewhere.
24.	Unfounded claims	A false hero presents unfounded claims.
25.	Difficult task	A difficult task is proposed to the hero.
26.	Solution	A difficult task is resolved.
27.	Recognition	The hero is recognized.
28.	Exposure	False hero or villain is exposed.
29.	Transfiguration	The hero is given a new appearance.
30.	Punishment	The villain is punished.
31.	Marriage	The hero is married and ascends the throne.

Propp's 31 Functions of Characters

His functions and a brief description of each are listed above. I should point out that most of his book is devoted to describing each function and often there are many variations for each function. All stories start, he says, with an initial situation in which the members of some "family" (or some entity, organization, etc.) are introduced. The initial situation is not a function according to Propp.

These 31 functions of Propp have to be updated to deal with contemporary stories, so the last function, the "hero is married and ascends the throne" might be changed to the "hero makes love with the woman he has saved from some villain." The reason these functions can be applied to contemporary texts is that Propp's functions are some of the primary activities that occur in stories: a villain does something, a hero is sent off to fight the villain, the hero gets some kind of magic agent (James Bond gets various "magic gizmos and gadgets" from Q) and so on.

When applying Propp to a text, we can use whichever of the 31 functions are applicable. What Propp reveals is that many narrative texts, contemporary and otherwise, have very strong fairy tale elements in them and that the fairy tale, with various disguises and modifications, is at the core of many narratives. There are, of course, some kinds of narratives that don't have many of Propp's elements in them, so we can't expect to use Propp for all narratives and some functions have to be modernized.

Propp also distinguished between two kinds of heroes: *victim heroes* (who directly experience villainy and then battle with villains) and *seekers heroes* (who go off in search of something that is lacking or to liquidate some misfortune). Both kinds of heroes receive magic agents. In modern texts, it is sometimes difficult to separate the two kinds of heroes, since seeker heroes are often victimized and victimized heroes often become seekers, but Propp argues that in folktales they are quite different.

What we will find is that many of Propp's functions are found in Shakespeare's comedies. *The Comedy of Errors* involves seekers and, since this is a comedy, they eventually find what they are seeking and there is a marriage or the equivalent of a marriage.

Paradigmatic Analysis of Texts

A paradigmatic analysis of a text looks at the pairs of binary oppositions found in it, such as good or evil, beautiful or ugly, happy or sad. While a syntagmatic analysis focuses on the sequence of events in a text and how the sequence generates meaning, a paradigmatic analysis focuses on how the binary oppositions hidden in the text generate meaning.

Figure 3.5 Claude Lévi-Strauss.

As Alan Dundes, a folklorist, wrote in his introduction to Propp's book, paradigmatic analysis (1968: xi):

> Seeks to describe the pattern (usually based upon an a priori binary principle of opposition) which allegedly underlies the folkloristic text. This pattern is not the same as the sequential structure at all. Rather the elements are taken out of the given order and are regrouped according to one or more analytic schema. [...] Levi-Strauss's position is essentially that the linear sequential structure is but apparent or manifest content, whereas the paradigmatic or schematic structure is the more important latent content.

Dundes argues that Lévi-Strauss related the paradigmatic structure he finds in myth to the world at large, and he sees myth and other forms of folklore as models that can be related to the world at large. This is like de Saussure's notion that concepts have meaning differentially and Roman Jakobson's argument that binary oppositions are the fundamental way the mind creates meaning.

For the work that I am presently doing involving humor in British, American, and Irish literature, Arthur Asa Berger has provided a very insightful and useful methodology for analyzing and creating humorous discourse in his *The Art of Comedy Writing*. For me, his model is as powerful as such other discourse models as "Script Model Grammar," by Raskin and others, "Conversational Implicatures," by Grice and others, "Conversational Analysis," by Tannen and others, "Genre and Archetype Theory," by Frye, White and others, "Signification Theory," by Henry Lewis Gates and others, "Dialogique Theory," by Bakhtin and others, various ethnographic and linguistic models by Schiffrin and others, or indeed any discourse model I have studied and/or used. Although Berger's model is flawed in many ways, and although it is presented in a glib fashion, it is nevertheless a powerful and rigorous model. Its power comes from its detail (45 techniques of devices) and its rigor comes from how this detail is spelled out (15 "Language" devices, 14 "Logic" devices, 13 "Identity" devices, and 3 "Action" devices).

Don L.F. Nilsen. *Journal of Humor Research* 1996:96–97.

Chapter 4

GLOSSARY: THE 45 TECHNIQUES OF HUMOR

The 45 Techniques of Humor

As the result of the research I conducted many years ago, on the techniques of humor, on what "makes us laugh," I came up with 45 techniques that, I argue, generate humor in everything from jokes and cartoons to dramatic comedies. I wrote a book, *The Art of Comedy Writing*, in which I use these 45 techniques to analyze dramatic comedies (plays) from Roman times to the present. When I finished my research, I had 45 techniques of humor, found in the tables that follow, that I soon realized could be classified in 4 ways: humor based on language, logic, identity and action. Visual aspects of comedy are covered in various techniques involving identity.

Table 4.1 Techniques of humor according to category.

LANGUAGE	LOGIC	IDENTITY	ACTION
Allusion	Absurdity	Before/After	Chase
Bombast	Accident	Burlesque	Slapstick
Definition	Analogy	Caricature	Speed
Exaggeration	Catalog	Eccentricity	
Facetiousness	Coincidence	Embarrassment	
Insults	Comparison	Exposure	
Infantilism	Disappointment	Grotesque	
Irony	Ignorance	Imitation	
Misunderstanding	Mistakes	Impersonation	
Over literalness	Repetition	Mimicry	
Puns/Wordplay	Reversal	Parody	
Repartee	Rigidity	Scale	
Ridicule	Theme/Variation	Stereotype	
Sarcasm	Unmasking		
Satire			

Then I enumerated them to make it easier to apply them to texts. Techniques numbered and in alphabetical order

Table 4.2 Techniques of humor in alphabetical order.

1. Absurdity	16. Embarrassment	31. Parody
2. Accident	17. Exaggeration	32. Puns
3. Allusion	18. Exposure	33. Repartee
4. Analogy	19. Facetiousness	34. Repetition
5. Before/After	20. Grotesque	35. Reversal
6. Bombast	21. Ignorance	36. Ridicule
7. Burlesque	22. Imitation	37. Rigidity
8. Caricature	23. Impersonation	38. Sarcasm
9. Catalog	24. Infantilism	39. Satire
10. Chase scene	25. Insults	40. Scale, Size
11. Coincidence	26. Irony	41. Slapstick
12. Comparison	27. Literalness	42. Speed
13. Definition	28. Mimicry	43. Stereotypes
14. Disappointment	29. Mistakes	44. Theme/Variation
15. Eccentricity	30. Misunderstanding	45. Unmasking

In my analysis of Shakespeare's play, I will offer examples of the 45 techniques that, I argue, generate humor, mirthful laughter and pleasure in his works. I offer a more detailed analysis (and examples) of the 45 techniques below. When we critique literary works (or in the current jargon "texts") we use the term "style" to represent what is distinctive and personal in an author's writing. We can also use the word "voice" to stand for the same thing. For great authors, this style or voice is easily recognizable; it has to do with how they use language, with their tone, and with how authors infuse their philosophy and knowledge about life into their works. Some authors adopt what might be described as "comedic style," namely the techniques they use to generate mirthful laughter. To determine comedic style, we have to know something about the techniques of humor, the subject of this chapter.

I believe that most of these techniques are self-explanatory, but I will briefly explain how I interpret each term, and, in most cases, offer examples. I suggest that the choices an author makes from the techniques and the way an author uses them allow us to define an author's style and understand the humor in a more granular way than is possible with the "why" theories of humor.

There are several things about my list of techniques that should be considered:

I have listed as techniques satire and parody, which many critics see as styles or genres rather than techniques. But I think we can argue that since, in common parlance, we talk about the way authors satirize and parody people and institutions, it isn't too much of a liberty to describe them as techniques.

The 45 techniques are generally found in combination. For example, an insult, which I list as a technique, is not in itself humorous but generates mirthful laughter only when the insult is combined with other humorous techniques, such as exaggeration, sarcasm and ridicule that it can be seen as funny. At times, it is difficult to decide which techniques are being used and whether one technique is basic.

Sometimes, the techniques can be reversed. Thus, if we turn insult humor on oneself, it becomes victim humor, and if we reverse exaggeration, it becomes an understatement. When several techniques are being used at the same time, it is difficult to determine which technique is dominant and most applicable to a given bit of dialogue or scene in a text. But with practice, this becomes easier.

These techniques tell us, in a granular fashion, what *makes* people laugh, but they do not tell us *why* people laugh or find something humorous. That is a subject about which there is a great deal of controversy. I argue that these 45 techniques have been used by everyone from Plautus and Shakespeare to Eugene Ionesco—that is, from ancient times to the present day. I also believe that they are universal.

It is necessary to assume a "play frame" in dealing with these techniques. Insults, for example, are not funny—except in a play frame in which we realize the insults are not serious and where make-believe, fantasy and imagination are part of the situation.

Many of the examples I use are taken from dramatic comedies, but each example is somewhat decontextualized and, in taking them from the scene in which they are found, the examples lose something. I try to supply some context to make the passages more understandable. Also, some quotes are rather extensive, to provide a sense of what the characters are like. But the examples, even if they are not always funny in themselves, enable us to see a technique in operation.

Just as we can use the techniques to analyze humor, we can use them to create humor, and that is what playwrights do when they write comedies—though, of course, it is unlikely (and in many cases impossible) that they know anything about my list of 45 techniques. But they know, one way or another, some of these techniques and use them, either consciously or intuitively, or, at times, in some combination of both.

With these considerations in mind, let us look at the 45 techniques of humor that, in various permutations and combinations, I suggest, are the basis of humor.

1. Absurdity *(logic)*

This involves experimenting with logic (as in *The Bald Soprano*), having fantastic characters who utter seemingly ridiculous statements, and works characterized by nonsense and confusion. Absurdity works by making light of the "demands" of logic and rationality.

> MR. SMITH: Here's a thing I don't understand. In the newspapers they always give the age of deceased persons but never the age of the newly born. It doesn't make sense.
> MRS. SMITH: I never thought of that.

Here we see one of the many places in *The Bald Soprano* where Ionesco plays around with logic. If newspapers give the age of people who die in obituaries, why don't they give the age of babies who are born in birth announcements? On the face of it, it seems logical, except that we all know the age of babies when they are born. This kind of experimenting with logic is what I have in mind when I characterize absurdity as a technique of humor. We cannot use it for other forms of humor which do not have that quality.

2. Accident (logic)

I define accidents as things like slips of the tongue, typographic errors that are amusing, and people slipping on banana peels. There is a difference between accidents, which are based on chance, and errors or mistakes, which are based on imprudence or ignorance.

The following joke is an example of a comic text based on an accident.

The bandaged priest

A priest was walking down the street when two hippies who knew him came over to say hello. He was heavily bandaged, so one hippie said: "How did you get hurt bad enough to require such a bandage?" "Oh, it was nothing," replied the priest. "I slipped in my bath. But it is fine now and no trouble." The hippies said they were sorry he was injured and walked away. A half-block down the street, the first hippie turned to the second and asked: "What's a bath?" A block later, the second hippie turned to the first and said, "How should I know? I ain't Catholic."

The joke involves the following elements (we can call them jokemes):

1. Two Hippies meet a priest.
2. The Hippies ask about his bandages.

3. The Priest explains he had an accident and slipped in his bath.
4. The Hippies leave the priest.
5. The first Hippie asks the second what a bath is.
6. The second Hippie says he doesn't know.
7. The second Hippie explains he isn't Catholic.

The humor is based on several techniques. First, it is based on an accident. Second, it uses *stereotypes* (identity), in this case, the popularly held notion that Hippies are dirty. Third, it uses the *revelation of ignorance* (logic); the first Hippie doesn't know what a bath is, and neither does the second hippie. Fourth, it has a *double-punch line* (language) that involves leading the listener on, for after the second Hippie says, "I don't know," we assume mistakenly that the joke is over. Then the second hippie says he isn't Catholic.

3. Allusion (language)

Allusions are one of the most common techniques of humor. Allusions often direct our attention to stupid things people have done, to scandals, to famous sexual liaisons (or to sex in general). One problem with understanding comedies from other cultures is that we don't "get" the allusions. The play is a *figure* and the society in which it is found is a *ground* or background and if we don't know this background, we miss much of the humor. In many early plays, for example, there are countless allusions to people and events that modern readers do not recognize or understand. Allusions depend upon people having background knowledge. This is necessary to understand the joke that follows.

A troupe of actors come to perform some plays by Shakespeare. The Sheriff of the county tells them they cannot advertise the plays they will be presenting. The director of the troupe puts a sign up at the theater and everyone knows what plays will be presented.

1. Wet   2. Dry   3. Miscarriage   4. three inches   5. six inches
6. nine inches

What were the plays?

1. Midsummer's Night Dream
2. Twelfth Night
3. Love's Labour Lost
4. Much Ado About Nothing
5. As You Like It
6. The Taming of the Shrew

Allusions often deal with sexual matters, personality traits, behavioral characteristics and other matters which are embarrassing, but not painful.

4. *Analogy, metaphor* (logic)

Analogies are comparisons and comic analogies are invidious ones that usually involve insult or ridicule. Metaphors and similes are common forms of figurative language that use analogies. Analogies by themselves are not humorous; they must be combined with other techniques of humor, such as insults and exaggeration to generate laughter. Consider this poem by Benjamin Franklin:

> Jack eating rotten cheese did say,
> Like Samson, I my thousands slay.
> I vow, quoth Roger, so you do.
> And with the self-same weapon, too.

The poem makes an analogy between Jack and Samson, who used the jawbone of an ass to slay people in a battle. You have to know this about Samson to make sense of the poem and recognize the aggression in it.

5. *Before and After* (Identity)

This technique, which I call "Before and After" deals with the transformations one often finds in humorous texts. Sometimes, an inept person is transformed into a sophisticated winner who triumphs over those who had previously made him or her a ridiculous figure. The changes (including the process by which the person is taught to be masterful) and what these changes lead to are the source of the humor. Or, a "winner" is transformed into an inept and defeated figure.

It is difficult to show this technique in a brief passage, but we find an example in Sheridan's *The School for Scandal*. Sir Peter Teazle is talking about his marriage to Lady Teazle.

> SIR PETER: When an old bachelor marries a young wife, what is he to expect? 'Tis now six months since Lady Teazle made me the happiest of men—and I have been the most miserable dog ever since!

Sir Peter is a senex figure, an older man who finds that being involved with a younger woman can be very problematic. In many comedies, an old senex figure wishes to marry a young woman and plots to do so but is foiled by the love interests of the woman.

6. **Bombast** (language)

Inflated language and rhetorical exuberance are the basis of bombast. The difference between what is said and the way it is said is one of the reasons we find bombast amusing. Another involves the skill of the person in using this inflated language. Here is an example from John Dryden's "Aurang Zebe."

> I burn, I more than burn; I am all fire,
> See how my mouth and nostrils flame, expire!
> I'll not come near myself.
> Now I am a burning lake, it rools and flows;
> I'll rush out and pour it upon my foes.

The language here is lyrical, elevated and exuberant, though there is also a comic aspect to it. It is often the disparity between the elevated language of bombast and its subject that generates the humor.

7. **Burlesque** (identity)

Burlesque refers to any literary form that makes individuals, social behavior or other literary works ridiculous by incongruously imitating them. It is a generic term that covers *satire* (which mocks society), *travesty* (which treats elevated literary works lowly) and *lampoon* (which ridicules individuals). Burlesque is perhaps the most problematic technique in this typology since it is a very broad and amorphous one and is used to cover many techniques, each of which has its own identity. Burlesque also refers to a kind of entertainment (at burlesque houses) that features striptease dancers and comedians who tell ribald and often crude jokes and take part in stupid and sophomoric humorous skits. I have included satire as a technique and consider travesty and lampoon as both subsumed under other techniques, such as ridicule and insult.

8. **Caricature** (identity)

Caricatures are drawings or other visual art forms in which a person's face is drawn exaggeratedly (yet the resemblance is kept) to ridicule the individual. Caricature is often used in political cartoons. Sir Thomas Browne wrote, in 1690, "When men's faces are drawn with resemblance to some other animals, the Italian's call it to be drawn in Caricaturia."

Self-caricature of the author as a superhero

The term caricature is usually used for comic drawings that exaggerate a person's features but maintain a resemblance, but it also can be used in portrayals that do the same thing. Although they are similar, I think it is possible to distinguish between caricature and mimicry.

9. *Catalogs* (logic)

I use the term catalog to involve lists that can use insult, wordplay, facetiousness and other techniques to obtain humorous effects. This listing or cataloging can be incorporated into dialogue in which a character lists things in response to questions from other characters; the random or incongruous nature of the items listed helps create the humor.

This catalog comes from F. Scott Fitzgerald's *The Great Gatsby*:

> From East Egg, then, came the Chester Bakers and the Leeches, a man named Bunsen, who I knew at Yale, and Doctor Webster Civet, who was drowned last summer up at Maine. And the Nornbeams and the Willie Voltaires, and a whole clan named Blackbuck, who always gathered in a corner and flipped up their noses like goats at whosoever came near. And the Ismays and the Christies (or rather Hubert Auerbach and Mr. Christie's wife), and Edgar Beaver, whose hair, they say, turned cottonwhite one afternoon for no good reason at all.

In this passage, Fitzgerald was satirizing "the beautiful people," and had fun turning them into animals like civets, leeches, hornbeams, goats and bucks.

10. Chase scenes (visual)

Chase scenes involve a character being chased, for one reason or another, by other characters (such as Buster Keaton being chased by thousands of policemen in *Cops*). The character who is chased uses ingenuity and various other ploys to escape capture. Keaton is not caught in *Cops*; after having been chased by an entire police force and eluding them, ironically, at the end of the film, having been spurned by the woman he loves, he turns himself in. Chase scenes aren't always humorous, of course; they are a standard dramatic technique used in serious (as opposed to humorous) dramas like James Bond movies, police adventures and thrillers.

11. Coincidences (logic)

As the result of chance, characters often find themselves in awkward, uncomfortable or embarrassing situations—which audiences find amusing. Coincidence is often paired with another technique, revelation and unmasking, in which characters who are pretending to be virtuous are shown for what they really are, or men who are pretending to be women are discovered. In Sheridan's *The School for Scandal*, there is a scene in which Joseph Surface, a man who pretends to be virtuous but is really a scoundrel, has lured Lady Teazle, the attractive young wife of Sir Peter Teazle, his potential benefactor, to his apartment. He intends to seduce her. Joseph is explaining that Lady Teazle suffers from too much virtue and that she should sin to preserve her reputation (Act IV, Scene 3).

JOSEPH:	Then, by this hand, which he is unworthy of-- [*Taking her hand*] Re-enter SERVANT 'Sdeath, you blockhead--what do you want?
SERVANT:	I beg your pardon, sir, but I thought you would not choose Sir Peter to come up without announcing him.
JOSEPH:	Sir Peter!--Oons--the devil!
LADY TEAZLE:	Sir Peter! O Lud! I'm ruined! I'm ruined!
SERVANT:	T'wasn't I let him in.
LADY TEAZLE:	Oh! I'm quite undone! What will become of me? Now, Mr. Logic--Oh! Mercy, sir, he's on the stairs--I'll get behind here--and if I'm ever so imprudent again---- [*Goes behind the screen*]

Sir Peter's arrival interrupts Joseph Surface's attempt to seduce Sir Peter's wife and leads to a situation where she hides and can overhear the conversation between Joseph and her husband. We have an example here of ignorance or discrepant awareness since Sir Peter does not know his wife is in the apartment, hidden behind a screen.

12. *Comparisons* (logic)

Analogies, mentioned earlier, involve comparisons, but they are indirect. They always involve metaphors or similes. Comparisons, as I use the term, are direct and use other techniques, such as insult or ridicule to generate their humor. Comparisons are odious, because most comparisons involve criticism of some kind, either directly or implicitly.

I offer two examples, one from real life.

I published a book many years ago titled *The TV-Guided American*. A reviewer of the book concluded his review of the book with:

> "Berger is to the study of television what Idi Amin is to tourism in Uganda."

Since Idi Amin, the president of Uganda, was killing thousands of people who opposed his rule, the comparison was truly odious. Another comparison, political in nature, follows:

> What's the difference between capitalism and communism? In capitalism, man exploits man. In communism, it is just the opposite.

In this text, we find ourselves with man exploiting man in both capitalism and communism because of the structure of the sentence.

13. *Definitions* (language)

Comic definitions are often used by humorists. Their definitions involve other techniques, such as insult, sarcasm and ridicule. We also find humorous definitions amusing because they involve defeated expectations—we expect something serious (since we associate definitions with dictionaries) and get something frivolous. In *Henry IV Part I* there is a famous definition of the term "honor" by Falstaff, as he responds to a statement by Hal: (Act V, Scene 2)

> PRINCE: Why, thou owest God a death. [Exit.]
> FALSTAFF: 'Tis not due yet: I would be loath to pay him before his day. What need I be so forward with him that calls not

on me? Well, 'tis no matter: honor pricks me on. Yea, but how if honor pricks me off when I come on? How then? Can honor set to a leg? No. Or an arm? No. Or take away the grief of a wound? No. Honor hath no skill at surgery then? No. What is honor? A word. What is that word honor? Air. A trim reckoning. Who hath it? He that died a Wednesday. Doth he feel it? No. Doth he hear it? No. 'Tis insensible then? Yea, to the dead. But will [it] not live with the living? No. Why? Detraction will not suffer it. Therefore I'll none of it. Honor is a mere scutcheon--and so ends my catechism. [Exit.]

This passage is not whimsical and full of laughs, though it has some wordplay in it. It helps establish the character of Falstaff as a realist (and perhaps a coward). As such, it is connected to an element of humor that recognizes what might be described as the profoundly absurd nature of life, in which people often, and sometimes foolishly, lay down their lives for mere "words."

14. *Disappointments and defeated expectations* (logic)

This technique, involving a person's expectations (often of a sexual nature) are led on and then, being denied at the last moment, because of an accident, coincidence, misunderstanding or something of that nature. Humor involving sexual frustration is very common in American culture according to sociologists who have studied the matter.

In Neil Simon's *Come Blow Your Horn*, there is a scene in which Alan, a 33-year-old bachelor, is expecting Peggy, a gorgeous woman, who lives above him, and with whom he has spent the weekend in Vermont, to come down to his apartment for a romantic liaison. Alan's brother Buddy is in Alan's apartment and is planning to move in, to get free from their dominating parents: a bossy father, for whom they both work, and a smothering mother.

BUDDY: You sure I won't be in your way here or anything?
(*Picking up his coat and suitcase.*)
ALAN: Of course not. We just may have to work out a traffic system. I've got a girl coming down in a few minutes.
BUDDY: A girl? Why didn't you say so? Whenever you want to be alone, just say the word. I'll go out to a movie.
ALAN: Don't worry. With my schedule, you won't miss a picture this year. (*The doorbell rings*) You hear that? She's here ten minutes ahead of time. (*The doorbell rings again*)

BUDDY: I'd better put this in here and go. (*Goes into the bedroom*)
ALAN: No, no. I want you to see her first. (*He crosses to door*) Ready for the thrill of your life? (*He opens the door a crack as he says:*) [...] and my third wish, O Geni, is that when I open the door, the most beautiful girl in the world will be standing there. (*He motions Buddy to come out of the bedroom. As he opens the door, there stands his FATHER, scowling disgustedly*) Dad!!

Alan thought it was Peggy and thus was surprised to see his father, as was his brother Buddy. It turns out that Alan uses the line "and my third wish, O Geni ..." several times, so we also have repetition and pattern as the play progresses. When he says "ready for the thrill of your life" he sets up the situation to be a major example of defeated expectations. Many disappointments in comedies involve frustrations people experience in trying to get alone and have the chance to make love.

15. *Eccentricity* (identity)

Writers use characters who are eccentric and bizarre, one way or another, to create humor. These eccentrics usually represent certain types—misers, misanthropes, drunkards, liars, braggarts, poseurs—who cannot control themselves and usually end up outsmarting themselves and learning painful lessons. In this respect, let us consider the hero of Samuel Beckett's *Krapp's Last Tape*. He reveals his eccentricity throughout the play, with his comments and his remarkable tapes, but there are several scenes of particular interest:

KRAPP: Good to be back in my den, in my old rags. Have just eaten I regret to say three bananas and only with difficulty refrained from a fourth. Fatal things for a man with my condition.

Then, a short while later, we find the following bit of dialogue from Krapp that gives more insight into his personality:

KRAPP: Statistics. Seventeen hundred hours, out of the preceding eight thousand odd, consumed on licensed premises alone. More than 20%, say 40% of his waking life. (*Pause*) Plans for a less (*hesitates*) [...] engrossing sexual life. Last illness of his father. Flagging pursuit of unattainable laxation. Sneers at what he calls his youth and thanks to God that it's over.

Beckett uses a telegraphic style to create his remarkable character, who, we must remember, is shown with a white face and a purple nose, suggesting to the audience that he is some kind of a clown figure.

16. *Embarrassment and escape from it* (identity)

Characters who find themselves in situations in which they are made to feel uncomfortable, ashamed, self-conscious, or ridiculous are embarrassed, as I use the term. They inevitably seek to escape from these situations and the events that lead to their embarrassments. Comedies frequently involve characters who get into messes and then do all kinds of things to get out of them, so the technique of embarrassment is of central importance.

In Neil Simon's *Come Blow Your Horn*, there is a scene in which Alan, a 33-year-old bachelor, has come back from a weekend with Peggy, a beautiful woman who lives in the same house. He is, we discover later, in love with another woman—Connie (Act I).

PEGGY: Why don't you come up in twenty minutes?
ALAN: Why don't you come down in nineteen?
PEGGY: All right. 'By, Alan.
ALAN: 'By, Connie.
PEGGY: Peggy! (*She breaks from him*)
ALAN: What?
PEGGY: Peggy! That's the third time this week you called me Connie.
ALAN: I didn't say Connie. I said Honey!
PEGGY: Oh!
ALAN: Oh!
PEGGY: Sorry.

Alan has made a mistake and finds himself in an embarrassing situation. He escapes from this embarrassment by using his wits, and saying he said "honey" instead of "Connie." In comedies, characters often make mistakes that put them in embarrassing situations and then have to work hard to escape from these embarrassments. Audiences take pleasure in the various comic mistakes, in the ensuing embarrassments, and in the ingenuity used to escape from these embarrassments.

17. *Exaggeration* (language)

By exaggeration, I mean enhancing reality and blowing things up far beyond the reality of the situation. Exaggeration is the technique found in "tall tales."

Exaggeration can also be reversed, leading to humorous understatement. Sometimes the exaggeration is direct, as in a description a person makes of some event or object; at other times, it is indirect, and we can see the person exaggerating. The joke about mosquitos in Alaska is an excellent example of the role of exaggeration in humor.

The mosquitos of Alaska

The mosquitos of Alaska are world famous for their size and ferocity. During the mosquito season in Alaska, no Alaskans go out at night, except in cars. One night, an unsuspecting visitor was seized by two gigantic mosquitos. "Shall we eat him here or take him to the swamp?" one mosquito asked the other. "Here," replied the other mosquito. "If we take him to the swamp, the big mosquitos will take him away from us."

18. *Exposure* (identity)

In exposure, characters inadvertently reveal something about themselves—often of a sexual nature—or sometimes, as the result of a mistake or coincidence, expose their bodies (they are shown naked or partly naked). We are amused when people who try to hide aspects of their sexual lives or who try to prevent their bodies from being seen are unsuccessful in doing so. At other times, characters are exposed as frauds, liars, cowards, impersonators and so on. We find a revelation of character in the scene described below, where Falstaff is shown exaggerating with wild abandon. Just after Falstaff has exaggerated the number of men he has killed, the Prince calls Falstaff's bluff (Act II, Scene 4):

> PRINCE: We two saw you four set on four, and bound them and were masters of their wealth. Mark now, how a plain tale shall put you down. Then did we two set on your four, and with a word, outfaced you from your prize, and have it; yea, and can show it you here in the house. And, Falstaff, you carried your guts away as nimbly, with as quick dexterity, and roared for mercy, and still run and roared, as ever I heard bullcalf. What a slave art thou to hack thy sword as thou hast done, and then say it was in fight! What trick, what device, what starting hole canst thou now find out to hide thee from this open and apparent shame?

Falstaff is thus exposed as a comic fraud, and in a play frame, exposing people who pretend to be what they are not or exposing people who are impersonating others is a source of humor. There is an element of comic tension generated involving exposure: will frauds be discovered? Much of the humor here involves discrepant awareness: a discrepancy between what some characters know and others don't or what the audience knows and what other characters don't know. A good deal of humor, as we shall see in my analyses of some classic plays, involves people pretending to be someone else or pretending to differ from the way they really are.

19. *Facetiousness* (language)

Facetiousness refers to a joking, frivolous, nonserious use of language and attitude by a character. The problem with being facetious is that it can easily be misunderstood; somehow the fact that one is being facetious must be made clear to one's audience. We see an excellent example of facetiousness in Falstaff's description of himself and his colleagues not as robbers but as "Diana's foresters." He is talking to Prince Hal (Act I, Scene 2).

> FALSTAFF: Marry, then, sweet wag, when thou art king let not us that are squires of the night's body be called thieves of the day's beauty. Let us be Diana's foresters, gentlemen of the shade, minions of the moon; and let men say we be men of good government, being governed as the sea is, by our noble and chaste mistress the moon, under whose countenance we steal.

Here Falstaff is being facetious and using language playfully to describe thieving as being one of Diana's foresters and thieves as being "minions of the moon."

20. *Grotesque* (identity)

A grotesque is a character who pushes the matter of eccentricity to almost painful ends. The grotesque isn't always comic, but if the grotesques are not physically deformed or terribly ugly and have elements about them, such as absurdity, single-mindedness and eccentricity, we see grotesques as comic. We can also use the term to apply to types of characters and situations. This passage from M. Bulgakov's novel, *The Master and the Margarita*, describes a grotesque:

> Just then the sultry air coagulated and wove itself into the shape of a man—a transparent man of the strangest appearance. On his small

head was a jockey cap, and he wore a short checked jacket fabricated of air. The man was seven feet tall but narrow in the shoulders, incredibly thin with a face made for derision.

Bulgakov's novel is considered a masterpiece of contemporary Russian fiction.

21. *Ignorance, gullibility, naiveté* (logic)

Ignorant characters who are gulls, fools, stupid and so on are found in many comedies. We find the revelation of ignorance by characters amusing (perhaps because we feel "superior" to these ignorant characters). We also find the "creation of ignorance" in a character who is deceived by other characters, such as an impersonator, amusing. There are, I would suggest, two kinds of comic ignorance: some characters are stupid and reveal their ignorance in the play's course, while others are "made" ignorant by being tricked or deceived by other characters.

This latter kind of ignorance has been termed "discrepant awareness" and is a major element in comedies. Sometimes, members of the audience know things that some characters don't know (that, for example, a certain character is a male pretending to be a woman). In other cases, the audience itself is made to experience "discrepant awareness" and doesn't know what one (or more) of the characters in the play knows.

Thus, in *Twelfth Night*, Malvolio, Olivia's steward, doesn't know that a letter he finds was not written by Olivia but by her maid, Maria, and is a forgery, part of a practical joke being played on him. And he does not know when he is prancing in Olivia's garden and talking to himself, that he is being overheard by Maria, Sir Toby Belch, Sir Andrew Aguecheek (two comic characters in their own right), and a servant, Fabian. They comment, to the audience, on Malvolio's statements (Act II, Scene 5).

MALVOLIO:	'Tis but fortune, all is fortune. Maria once told me she did affect me. And I have heard herself come thus near, that, should she fancy, it should be one of my complexion. Besides, she uses me with a more exalted respect than anyone else that follows her. What should I think on 't?
SIR TOBY:	Here's an overweening rogue!
FABIAN:	Oh, peace! Contemplation makes a rare Turkeycock of him. How he jets under his advanced plumes!
SIR ANDREW:	'Slight, I could so beat the rogue!
SIR TOBY:	Peace, I say.

MALVOLIO:	To be Count Malvolio.
SIR TOBY:	Ah, rogue!
SIR ANDREW:	Pistol him, pistol him.
SIR TOBY:	Peace, peace!
MALVOLIO:	There is an example for 't. The lady of Strachy married the yeoman of the wardrobe.
SIR ANDREW:	Fie on him, Jezebel!
FABIAN:	Oh, peace! Now he's deeply in. Look how imagination blows him.
MALVOLIO:	Having been three months married to her, sitting in my state--
SIR TOBY:	Oh, for a stonebow, to hit him in the eye!
MALVOLIO:	Calling my officers about me, in my branched velvet gown, having come from a day bed, where I have left Olivia sleeping--

This scene is a classic example of ignorance or discrepant awareness. It is one in which people who are being talked about are hidden and overhear what is said about them while the speaker is unaware that this is the case. Often, in such situations, the speaker says insulting things about those who are hidden. Thus, the speaker ridicules those who are hiding, but the speaker is also being ridiculed for not knowing his or her words are being overheard.

22. *Imitation and pretense* (identity)

Imitation, as I use the term, involves a character pretending to be something else—a dog, a chair, a robot (as in Woody Allen's *Sleepers*) or to be in a different state (a dying man, as in *Volpone*). In *Volpone*, at the end of Act I, Scene 2, Volpone describes the situation, as Mosca exits, to bring in Voltore:

> VOLPONE: Now, my feigned cough, my phthisis, and my gout,
> My apoplexy, palsy, and catarrhs,
> Help, with your forced functions, this my posture,
> Wherein, this three years, I have milked their hopes.
> He comes, I hear him--uh! uh! uh! uh! O--

Volpone then imitates a dying man when Voltore comes in and says things like:

> VOLPONE: I feel me going, uh! uh! uh! uh!
> I am sailing to my port, uh! uh! uh! uh!

Mosca tells Voltore he will inherit everything of Volpone's, which is what Mosca tells all the people who bring Volpone gifts, hoping to get on his good side and to inherit all his wealth.

23. *Impersonation* (identity)

I differentiate between imitation and impersonation. Imitation, as I have just suggested, involves a character pretending to be something else. Impersonation involves a character taking on someone else's identity or a profession (such as a doctor). The impersonator often "degrades" the character being impersonated (or the profession). There is always a tension created—will the impersonator be discovered? There is also the question as to what mischief the impersonator will accomplish. In *Twelfth Night*, after Malvolio has been locked up because he is thought to be mad, the clown puts on a gown and pretends to be Sir Topas, the curate.

>   [Enter MARIA and CLOWN.]
> MARIA: Nay, I put on this gown and this beard. Make him believe you art Sir Topas the curate. Do it quickly. I'll call Sir Toby the whilst. [exit.]
> CLOWN: Well, I'll put it on, and I will dissemble myself in't, and I would I were the first that ever dissembled in such a gown.

A short while later, the Clown, dressed as Sir Topas, visits Malvolio, who is in a dark dungeon. This leads to a conversation between Malvolio and the Clown, who is impersonating Sir Topas.

> MALVOLIO: [*Within*] Who calls there?
> CLOWN: Sir Topas the curate, who comes to visit Malvolio the lunatic.
> MALVOLIO: Sir Topas, Sir Topas, good Sir Topas, go to my lady.
> CLOWN: Out, hyperbolical fiend. How vexst thou this man! Talkest thou nothing but of ladies?

The conversation continues on, with Malvolio not recognizing that he's been fooled, another example of ignorance and discrepant awareness. Imitation must involve a kind of ignorance on the part of some characters, who, for example, when they are attracted to men pretending to be women, make fools of themselves. Of course, in comedies, characters are always making fools of themselves—one way or another.

GLOSSARY

24. *Infantilism* (language)

Infantilism, as I interpret the term, involves an adult character using the language of a baby and experimenting with words, uttering nonsense terms and the like. Let me offer a brief example from Ionesco's *The Bald Soprano*.

MRS. SMITH:	Mice have lice, lice haven't mice.
MRS. MARTIN:	Don't ruche my brooch!
MRS. SMITH:	Don't smooch the brooch!
MRS. MARTIN:	Groom the goose, don't goose the groom.

This dialogue also uses repetition and pattern and is similar to the language of infants, as they learn how to experiment with sounds, often making nonsensical sounds in the process.

25. *Insults* (language)

A humorous insult is a direct use of verbal aggression to degrade a person or some other object (such as an institution) for comic effect. Insults often involve wild comparisons, attacks on sexual aspects of a person, allusions to embarrassing things done in the past and with so on. Insults are not humorous in themselves, so they must use other techniques to create the humor and the insulter must make certain that the insults are not seen as "real," but are tied to a role in a play or as part of one's actions or something like that. (That is, there must be a play frame.) Insults are very dangerous ways to generate laughter but are commonly used. Insults that are reversed and directed at oneself yield "victim" humor.

In *Travesties*, Stoppard makes good use of comic insults in several places. In one scene, Carr, the central character of the play, insults Tzara:

> CARR: My God, you little Rumanian wog--you bloody dago
> --you jumped-up phrase-making smart-alecky
> arty-intellectual Balkan turd!!! Think you
> know it all!--while we poor dupes
> think we're fighting for ideals, you've got a
> profound understanding of what is *really* going on,
> underneath,

Stoppard is using comic insult here to delineate Tzara. Comic insults are found in many humorous texts, sometimes directed at particular individuals with whom one is conversing, but at other times are directed at characters in a play who are not on stage when the insults are made (but who may overhear them). At other times, insults are directed at institutions, kinds of people (parents, children and mothers-in-law), occupations (psychiatrists, professors, priests, rock stars, etc.), nationalities, religions and so on.

26. *Irony* (language)

Eirons, characters who are wise and pretend to be dumb, powerful and pretend to be weak, or deceitful but pretend to be honest, are stock figures in comedy. Irony is a very complicated subject. Verbal irony involves saying one thing but meaning the opposite (and trying to make sure that your real meaning is understood). Dramatic irony refers to situations in plots: a character pursues some goal but gets the opposite of what he or she seeks.

The following joke is an example of irony:

> A Jewish man named Katzman decides to change his name to a French name so people wouldn't be able to recognize that he was Jewish. He goes to a judge for help. "French," you say," says the judge. "Well, the French word for cat is chat and the French word for man is l'homme. We will change your name to Chat-l-Homme."

One problem with irony is that sometimes people do not recognize that something said is ironic. They don't "get" the irony and take what is said ironically in a literal way, so irony is dangerous. The irony in the joke is that Katzman ends up with a name that is even more Jewish since his French-sounding name sounds like shalom, the Hebrew word for "hello."

27. *Literalness* (language)

Literalness, or more correctly over-literalness, is the basis of moron jokes and much comedy. It involves characters who are stupid and take everything literally or who lack imagination and good sense—who are not flexible and who do not take circumstances into account. As Bergon defines laughter as "something mechanical encrusted on the living," and also wrote, "A comic effect is obtained whenever we pretend to take literally an expression which was used figuratively."

> Why did the moron take a ladder to the party?
> Because he heard the drinks were on the house.

> A man walked into a clothing store. "What can I do for you?" asked a clerk. "I'd like to try on that suit in the window," the man said. "We'd prefer you to use the dressing room," replied the clerk.

The humor of literalness is based on the inability of a character to take circumstances into account and interpret something said in a reasonable manner. There is also the matter of stupidity and misunderstanding that is often found in this kind of humor.

28. *Mimicry* (identity)

In mimicry, a person maintains his own identity but imitates the voice and language use of some famous individual such as Jimmy Stewart, John Wayne, Richard Nixon and so on. The mimic also uses other techniques to generate the humor: body language, facial expressions and allusions to embarrassing events, ridicule and the revelation of ignorance, insults and with so on. We see Shakespeare using this technique in *Henry IV Part I* (Act II, Scene 4) where Henry, the Prince of Wales, mimics both Hotspur and his wife:

> PRINCE: I am not yet of Percy's mind, the Hotspur of the North, he that kills me some six or seven dozen Scots at a breakfast, washes his hands, and says to his wife, "Fie upon this quiet life! I want work." "Oh my sweet Harry," says she, "how many hast thou killed today?" "Give my roan horse a drench," says he, and answers, "Some fourteen," an hour after; "a trifle, a trifle."

Harry does this by exaggerating Hotspur's exploits and imitating the way his wife speaks to him.

29. *Mistakes* (logic)

A mistake involves something one does, an error based on things such as poor judgment, inattention, inadequate information or stupidity. Mistakes are one of the fundamental techniques found in comedy, which involves various kinds of stupid and silly errors. I differentiate between mistakes and misunderstandings, which are verbal in nature.

Mistakes, of course, are only funny if there is a comic "play frame" around them. In the sitcom, *Frasier*, at the end of a scene Frasier asks Roz, his producer, how his first show went.

> *He gets up and enters Roz's booth. She is busy with administrative stuff.*
>
> FRASIER
> It was a good show, wasn't it?
> ROZ

> [*tears him a piece of notepaper*] Here, your brother called.
> ### FRASIER
> Roz, in the trade we call that "avoidance." Don't change the subject, tell me what you think.
> ### ROZ
> [*points at her console*] Did I ever tell you what this little button does?
> ### FRASIER
> I'm not a piece of Lalique. I can handle criticism. How was I today?
> ### ROZ
> Let's see. You dropped two commercials, you left a total of 28 seconds of dead air, you scrambled the station's call letters, you spilled yogurt on the control board, and you kept referring to Jerry with the identity crisis as "Jeff."

This bit of dialogue was accompanied by certain actions and facial expressions from Roz and reaction shots of Frasier that heightened its comic aspects. Frasier is revealed, almost immediately in the first episode, as something of a klutz, a bumbler prone to making mistakes. There is an element of irony in that Frasier, technically speaking a comedic fool, is a somewhat pompous and stuffy radio psychiatrist, who earns his living advising people who call him about their problems.

30. Misunderstanding (language)

As I suggested above, mistakes are based on things people do while misunderstandings are, as I see things, primarily verbal and involve characters not communicating effectively with one another. A misunderstanding is linguistic; nevertheless, it still is part of what might be described as the comedy of errors.

> A woman goes to a lawyer and says she wants to divorce her husband. "Do you have grounds?" asks the lawyer. "Yes," she replies. "Six acres." "Do you have a grudge?" asks the lawyer? "No," says the woman. "We have a carport." "I'd better get more specific, thinks the lawyer. "Does he beat you?" asks the lawyer. "No," says the woman. "I get up before he does." "Well, why do you want to get a divorce?" asks the lawyer. "Because my husband doesn't understand me," replies the woman.

The punchline shows that the woman cannot understand anyone, so there is something ironic about her wanting to divorce her husband.

31. *Parody* (identity)

Parody is a form of verbal mimicry in which the style and mannerisms of a well-known writer, such as Ernest Hemingway (parody of style), of a popular genre (such as a soap opera), or a famous text (James Bond novels), are imitated humorously. One problem with parody is that audiences must be familiar with the original text that is being parodied to get full enjoyment out of the parody, though audiences who don't know the text being parodied often can enjoy the parody as a humorous work in itself.

In "Spring Bulletin" Woody Allen parodies the style of writing found in college bulletins.

Introduction to psychology:

The theory of human behavior. Why some men are called "lovely individuals" and why there are others you just want to pinch. Is there a split between mind and body, and, if so, which is better to have? Aggression and rebellion are discussed. (Students particularly interested in these aspects of psychology are advised to take one of the Winter Term courses: Introduction to Hostility; Intermediate Hostility; Advanced Hatred; Theoretical Foundations of Loathing.) Special consideration is given to a study of consciousness as opposed to unconsciousness, with many helpful hints on how to remain conscious.

In this passage, Allen is parodying the way courses are described in university bulletins. We see that parody also involves other techniques of humor, such as ridicule and playing with logic to achieve the desired comedic effect.

32. *Puns, wordplay and other amalgamations* (language)

Puns and wordplay involve the clever use of language to amuse and entertain. Puns are a specific form that uses a word's sound to mean two different things. Wordplay involves wit, clever comments relative to some situations that are made in a timely manner. You cannot miss a beat if the witty comment is to be effective. We find puns and wordplay in many comedies; they are one of the most widely used techniques of linguistic humor.

> An English wit couldn't help himself and made puns on all occasions. On being taken to a bakery, he said "a bun is the lowest form of wheat." Finally, his friends thought they could silence him by taking him to see the Grand Canyon. He gazed at it for a moment and said, "Gorge-ous, isn't it."

In this joke, we have a reference to the commonly uttered statement, "the pun is the lowest form of wit." This statement is a bad overgeneralization because a good pun is a valid form of humor. It is the bad puns that are so distasteful.

33. *Repartee* (language)

Repartee, as I understand it, involves a character responding to slights, put-downs and veiled insults in a witty or clever manner. Repartee can make use of wordplay, allusion, odious comparison or other techniques of humor, but it must be timed perfectly, not missing a beat after the original provocation. Wit involves making clever comments at a moment's notice, but isn't necessarily negative or insulting and isn't, like repartee, a response to some kind of slight by someone. Repartee, thus, differs from wit, though a good repartee should be witty.

Isadora Duncan is reputed to have written to George Bernard Shaw, suggesting they breed together in the interest of eugenics. "Just imagine," she supposedly wrote, "of a child with my body and your brains." "Yes, madam, but what of a child with my body and your brains?" Shaw supposedly replied.

Repartee is a form of verbal dueling in which the game is to rebut an insult with a better insult or a statement with a more witty response. Time is critical because the repartee must be made immediately, which suggests that the repartee is connected to wit.

34. *Repetition and pattern* (logic)

Repetition involves the humor of iteration and the ability of characters to cope with situations that repeat themselves and often deal with characters who have monomaniacal characteristics. Running gags are a good example of repetition and pattern: Jack Benny nursed his definition of himself as a "cheapskate" for many years. We know, more or less, what the pattern is, but we don't know how the characters will find some new way to deal with it.

> A hunter's car broke down in the middle of nowhere. After walking for a few miles, he found a log cabin in the woods in which a settler and his wife and their three children lived. The hunter was fed very well and started feeling drowsy. The settler asked him to stay with them and the hunter accepted. "You'll have to wait a bit while I put the children to bed," said the settler. They were all put to bed and

when the last one was asleep, the settler lifted them one by one and laid on the floor in the back of the room. "She's all yours now," said the settler. The hunter protested but was persuaded. Because of his exhaustion, he fell immediately into a deep sleep. When he woke up, he was also on the floor with the kids and the settler and his wife were in the bed.

The humor of repetition is based on the tension created by the establishment of some kind of a series being established and our curiosity about whether it will be continued or some interesting variation on the repetition will be introduced.

35. *Reversal* (logic)

Reversal and contradiction involve things turning out differently from the way characters expect them to turn out. Sometimes, characters get even with those who have tormented them, and in other cases, characters outsmart themselves and get a bit of their own medicine. Generally, reversal is a consequence of exposure and revelation and involves irony on the level of plot and behavior—though it also can be seen in language and dialogue.

For an example of linguistic reversal, let us look at Wilde's *The Importance of Being Earnest*. Jack has proposed to his love, Gwendolyn (Act I):

> GWENDOLYN: Ernest, we may never be married. From the expression on mamma's face, I fear we never shall. Few parents nowadays pay any regard to what their children say to them. The old-fashioned respect for the young is fast dying out.

I see this as reversal rather than irony, which is an indirect or implied form of a reversal. In irony, you mean the opposite of what you say; in reversal, you twist conventional logic and speech around. Thus, conventionally we say children don't pay regard to what their parents tell them and the old-fashioned respect by the young for the old is dying out; by reversing things, Wilde makes a humorous comment on society and its values.

36. *Ridicule* (language)

Ridicule involves "making fun" and casting contemptuous laughter at someone or something. That is, we make individuals or institutions (or whatever) seem "ridiculous" which is what Aristotle argued is the basis of comedy.

In *The Importance of Being Earnest*, Wilde ridicules the image of the young gentry as being idle and ignorant. We find this in a conversation between Jack and Lady Bracknell:

BRACKNELL: Do you smoke?
JACK: Well, yes, I must admit I smoke.
BRACKNELL: I am glad to hear it. A man should always have an occupation of some kind. There are far too many idle men in London as it is. How old are you?
JACK: Twenty-nine.
BRACKNELL: A very good age to be married at. I have always been of the opinion that a man who desires to get married should know either everything or nothing. Which do you know?
JACK: [*After some hesitation.*] I know nothing, Lady Bracknell.
BRACKNELL: I am pleased to hear it. I do not approve of anything that tampers with natural ignorance. Ignorance is like a delicate exotic fruit; touch it and the bloom is gone. The whole theory of modern education is radically unsound. Fortunately in England, at any rate, education produces no effect whatsoever. If it did, it would prove a serious danger to the upper classes and probably lead to acts of violence in Grosvenor Square.

Wilde, through Lady Bracknell, is gently ridiculing English society and the supposedly idle wealthy classes. Ridicule is a form of humorous attack on a person, a thing, an institution, or an idea designed to generate contemptuous laughter and humiliation.

37. **Rigidity** (logic)

I use the term rigidity to characterize people who are undeviating in their performance of certain kinds of behavior, who are unbending and dominated by an idée fixe or ruling passion. Bergson argued that the basis of comedy involves "the mechanical encrusted on the living" and it is rigidity that may be seen as another term for mechanical. Much comedy involves characters who are locked in their roles as impostors, buffoons, braggarts, misers, cowards and so on.

38. **Sarcasm** (language)

Sarcasm means "tearing the flesh" or "biting the lips in rage" and refers to the use of language that is contemptuous, mocking and wounding. Sarcastic remarks are not directly insulting but are obliquely so, remarks that, by their tone, taunt and ridicule. They are often bitter, cutting, caustic and often extremely hostile.

> A woman's car stalls at a corner and remained there while the light turned red, yellow, and green several times. Finally, a traffic cop came up to her and said, "What's the matter, lady? Don't we have any colors you like?"

The manner of delivery of sarcasm is important since we must recognize from the tone of voice of the speakers that they are being sarcastic. Many people use sarcasm as an everyday stance in dealing with others, which can be seen as a kind of defense mechanism and a way of dealing with hostile and aggressive feelings.

39. Satire (language)

Defining satire is a very difficult and controversial matter. For our purposes, we will consider satire to be a technique that involves deriding and ridiculing stupidity, vice and folly in individuals, institutions and society. There is often an implicit moral dimension to satire; by pointing out how foolish we frequently are, it suggests that alternatives to the status quo should be considered.

In my book, *Li'l Abner: A Study in American Satire*, I quote from Capp's satirization of gourmandism. Bounder J. Roundheels has been trying to join the "Gourmet's Club" for many years and has been rejected nine times by P. Fangsgood Droolsby, the head of the club. The following passage takes place after the last rejection of Roundheels.

ROUNDHEELS:	Life isn't worth LIVING unless I can get into the "Gourmet's" Club!! It's the world's most exclusive organization of lovers of unique food. A vacancy occurred in 1909 when a member STARVED to death because there was nothing left in the world good enough for him to eat!!
ABNER:	Tsk! Tsk!! Hard t' PLEASE, huh?.... Yo' got ONE mo' chance, huh? You gotta whip up somethin' unusual THIS time—huh, Roundheels?
ROUNDHEELS:	YES, just ONE!! Ah yes!! They LAUGHED at my "heart of ripened century plant salad!!" They coldly BURPED at my "jellied armadillo brains with unborn mushrooms"

The episode concludes as follows: Roundheels cannot get a rare ingredient for his concoction, so has himself boiled down into a drop for his ecstasy sauce for a meal and is accepted into the club, but it is too late. Capp's strip is full of satires of many aspects of everyday life in America and was popular for years.

Northrop Frye, in his *Anatomy of Criticism*, suggests there are three kinds of satires:

Horation satire that is genial and attacks typical foibles and follies.
Juvenalian satire is savage in its condemnation of error and misbehavior.
Menippean satire that deals less with people than with mental attitudes. Pedants, bigots, cranks parvenus, virtuosi, enthusiasts, rapacious and incompetent professional men of all kinds, are handled in terms of their occupational approach to life as distinct from their social behavior.

It would seem that Capp is a Menippean satirist since his strips are full of the kind of people that Frye writes about.

40. *Scale* (identity)

Scale can be used to create humor by contrasting characters in size and involving them in ridiculous situations or using objects that are either much too large or too small for the purposes at hand. *Gulliver's Travels* involves scale, with Gulliver being "gigantic," when compared to the Lilliputians found in the book.

41. *Slapstick* (visual)

Slapstick is a physical form of comedy that involves things like characters having pies thrown in their faces, getting hit by mops, collisions between characters, slips on banana peels or greasy surfaces, comic fights and the destruction of objects (cars being torn apart, houses dismantled, etc.). Slapstick is considered "crude" but it is a very common technique of comedy, and as practiced by artists such as Chaplin or Laurel and Hardy, often was hilarious. Slapstick involves various forms of physical actions that we find amusing. It is an attack on our claims to adulthood, seriousness, importance and an elevated status of any kind. I consider comic violence a form of slapstick.

42. *Speed* (visual)

If we speed up certain actions, such as the way characters run in chase scenes or the way characters speak, these behaviors take on a humorous dimension.

The reverse also applies, in which actions are slowed down to an intolerable pace and made ridiculous.

43. Stereotypes (identity)

A stereotype is a commonly held view about the characteristics and typical behavior patterns of some group of people based on matters such as ethnicity, race, nationality and religion (Poles, Jews, WASPS, African-Americans and Russians). Stereotypes can be positive, negative or mixed—but generally, they are negative when used by humorists. Northrop Frye writes in his *Anatomy of Criticism*, about stock types who often function as stereotypes (1957:172):

> The *Tractatus* lists three types of comic characters: the *alazons* or impostors, the *eirons* or self-deprecators, and the buffoons (bomolochoi). This list is closely related to a passage in the Ethics which contrasts the first two and then goes on to contrast the buffoon with a character whom Aristotle calls *agroikos* or churlish, literally rustic. We may reasonably accept the churl as a fourth comic type, and so we have two opposed pairs. The contest of the *eiron* and *alazon* forms the basis of the comic action and the buffoon and churl polarize the comic mood.

The stock types often form the basis of stereotypes in humorous texts. We find stereotyping employed in Trevor Griffiths' play, *Comedians*, which is about an evening school course in comedy held in a secondary school in Manchester, England. The course is taught by Eddie Waters, and in the first act, while having a conversation with the students, Waters offers some stereotypes to show his students something about this technique and the nature of comedy. Waters asks the students to say a tongue twister, rapidly, "The traitor distrusts the truth." The students say the phrase, in turn, ending with one student, Price, who says (Act IOne):

> PRICE: The traitor distrusts truth.
> WATERS: (*Finally, mild, matter-of-fact*): I've never liked the Irish, you know. Dr. Johnson said they were a very truthful race, they never spoke well of each other, but then how could they have? (*They look around, faintly puzzled, amused.*) Big, thick, stupid heads, large cabbage ears, hairy nostrils, daft eyes, fat, flapping hands, stinking of soil and Guinness. The niggers of Europe. Huge, uncontrollable wangers, spawning their degenerate kind wherever they're allowed to settle. I'd stop them settling here if I had my way. Send 'em back to the primordial bog they came from. Potato heads.

In comedies, we find many stereotyped figures because they provide an instant "explanation" of motivation and because they lend themselves beautifully to ridicule, insult, exaggeration and other techniques as well.

We find stereotypes in a common kind of joke which makes fun of the behavior of people from different countries in certain situations.

> Two men and a young woman are shipwrecked on a desert island. If the men are French, one man will become the woman's husband and the other her lover. If they are Spanish, the men will fight a duel and whoever survives gets the girl. If they are English, nothing will happen because nobody is there to introduce them to one another. If they are Italian, one will murder the other to have the woman for himself. If they are Greek, they will get into an argument about politics and forget about the woman.

These jokes play with ideas and stereotypes people have of what members of different nationalities are like.

44. *Theme and variation* (logic)

By theme and variation, I refer to the technique comedy writers use to take some matter (a belief, an activity) and show how different nationalities, religions, occupations, members of social classes, etc. vary concerning this belief or activity. Part of the humor here comes from seeing how the theme is varied by the different plays with stereotypes people have of different groups.

> An American professor met three members of the Academie Francaise in Paris and asked them for their definition of savoir-faire. "This is not difficult," said one of the members. "If I go home and find my wife kissing another man and I tip my hat to them and say 'excuse me,' that is savoir-faire." "No, not really," said the second. "If I got home and find my wife kissing another man and say 'continue,' that is savoir-faire." "No, not yet," said the third. "If I go home and find my wife kissing another man and tip my hat and say 'excuse me, but please continue,' and he can continue, he has savoir-faire."

This kind of humor makes its basic appeal to logic and focuses upon the relativity of things and how people vary in the way they respond to situations in which they find themselves. The technique in itself is not humorous and must be used with other techniques of humor to generate mirthful laughter.

45. *Unmasking and pretense* (identity)

In unmasking, we bring to light what someone is trying to conceal (a secret, an identity or whatever). Pretense is the other side of the matter and involves a situation in which a character pretends something (a woman pretends she's a man or vice versa or a character pretends to be ill) to trick or fool other characters. When there is pretense, tension is established. Will the pretender be able to fool the other characters, or will he or she be unmasked? And if there is an unmasking, how is it accomplished?

> A handsome young businessman stationed in Tokyo came to America on a trip where he met a lovely young woman who he courted and married. "You'll love Tokyo," he told his wife. "I have a servant, Yamaka, who does everything. We'll have a wonderful time." When they arrived in Tokyo, the young businessman introduced the girl to Yamaka, who bowed and retired. The next morning, the young man said to his wife, "I have to go to the office but you can continue to sleep. Don't worry. Yamaka will take care of everything." Several hours later the young wife was nudged gently by Yamaka. "Okay missee, time to go home now."

Basic to unmasking is the revelation of something about someone that may be embarrassing and humiliating, but not serious.

Basic Techniques of Humor Generation and Style

From my perspective, one of the defining aspects of style is the way writers use and combine the various techniques of humor discussed in this glossary. These techniques, as I have pointed out, are often used in combination. In analyzing a simple text, such as a joke, it is quite common to find two or three techniques being used, with one technique dominant and other techniques having secondary status. With this list of techniques, it is possible to see how authors generate humor and determine whether an author tends to use certain techniques most of the time and neglect others. This use of particular techniques would give us, then, a more specific understanding of his or her comedic style than was possible before.

If you wish to be mechanistic, you can think of these techniques as "devices" used by authors. I don't believe that authors are conscious or fully conscious of the techniques they are using or that they can articulate them with any degree of precision. They create comedy based on a variety of factors, some conscious and others unconscious—what they feel is correct or "works" in a situation, to generate laughter and do whatever else they wish to do, at the same time. But armed with this catalog of techniques, we can see what techniques they have favored and can unravel, to some degree, the mystery of creating comedy.

On performance and theatrical matters

This book deals with dramatic comedies and thus does not consider the matter of performance in detail, but I would like to say something about it. There is a kind of magic in the way actors and actresses can "become" characters in plays and the way their performances can generate laughter. When we read plays and read stage directions, we can, in our mind's eye, often "see" the performances the authors expected. And, sometimes, when we've seen a play performed, we can remember the way the actors and actresses brought the play to life.

Below are some factors involved in performances that can be used to make the lines of a comedy do a better job of generating laughter. Many of these comic ploys involve using various techniques, such as exaggeration and imitation, I might add.

1. *Facial expression.* Performers can make "funny" faces to create humor, exaggerate their facial responses to lines or actions by other characters and use their faces (eyes, eyebrows, cheeks and lips) to reveal their feelings and attitudes.
2. *Body language.* Performers can use exaggerated body language to heighten the humor in a situation. They can jump, they can twist themselves into shapes, they can do "funny walking" and other things as well.
3. *Makeup and props.* The makeup of performers, their hairstyles and hair color, the clothes they wear and the props they use (their eyeglasses, for instance) all can contribute to the humor by suggesting character and personality. A grotesque character with a white face and a purple nose, like Krapp, affects people in the audience and colors, literally as well as figuratively, the way they react to him.
4. *Voice usage.* The way characters talk—in monotones, in high-pitched tones (when men pretend to be women), the accents and dialects they use and whether they talk very slowly or very quickly, speak correctly or incorrectly, talk gibberish and double-talk—all have comic potentialities.
5. *Noises and sound effects.* Here I'm talking about everything from belches and farts by uncouth characters to the use of noises (sirens, buzzers, telephones ringing, etc.) and other sound effects to heighten dramatic effects.
6. *Scenery.* Scenery can also intensify the comedic possibilities in a script—since it can be used to "reveal" what a character is really like (a slob, a fanatic about cleanliness, an aesthete, a square, a lecher).

A Note on Personality Types in Comedies

Aristotle said that comedy involved "an imitation of men worse than average," of people who are "ridiculous." The humorous characters in comedies often are "types"—monomaniacs, characters with one dominating humor or comic passion. These comic characters often are played off against relatively normal characters—frequently young lovers. They must cope with humorous characters of all sorts and find a way to use and manipulate their ruling passions to overcome the various obstacles these monomaniacs create for them.

A list of some of the more common types of humorous stock characters follows below.

1. *Boasters or Alazons*

We see them in everything from Greek comedies to modern-day works. One of the most famous is Miles Gloriosus, the boaster (and fool) in Plautus's play *Miles Gloriosus*. He lacks self-understanding and doesn't realize that everyone thinks of him as a fool. He is also a gull, who is naïve and easily persuaded, two common characteristics of fools.

2. *Pretenders or Eirons*

These characters trick other characters to achieve some goal: money, freedom, a loved one or a lusted after one, etc. A great deal of comedy involves characters who are dissemblers, pretending something (men pretending they are women, women pretending they are men, kings pretending they are commoners, servants pretending they are helping their masters and so on). Wily servants are often eirons.

3. *Gulls*

They are the naïve characters who are fooled by the pretenders and are tricked out of something.

4. *Hicks or Agroikos*

They are country bumpkins who know little of city life, are often gulls, though not always—since there is also the reverse—the convention of the shrewd country type who tricks gullible and naïve city types.

5. *Pedants*

In Commedia Dell'Arte, one of the standard characters is the dottore or pedant. These characters always have their nose buried in books and are unworldly and impractical, full of theoretical knowledge, but bumblers who cannot function in the real world. The stereotype of the absent-minded and unworldly professor comes from the dottore figure.

6. *Old men or senexe*

Frequently these characters have a beautiful young women who is their ward who is their ward and who, often, they wish to marry (or wish to marry off to someone the ward doesn't like) and it is the task of the hero, the male lead, often helped by a shrewd servant or slave (or similar figure) to outwit the *senex* and marry the girl.

7. *Fools or schlemiels*

Fools are people who lack self-knowledge, who are simpletons, who have bad luck, who are misfits, who are gauche, who make stupid bargains (can be gulled) and who are born losers and victims. (There are also wise fools in some plays—characters who know and speak the truth and, ironically, aren't listened to because they are fools.) In Jewish humor, there are many schlemiels who are inept and always spilling soup and when they spill soup, they always do so on characters who are even more gauche, schlimazels.

There are many other types such as dandies, fops, misers, misanthropes, sex-starved women and men, gluttons, cynics and milquetoasts, who are found in comedies. The common characteristic of many of these characters is that they are driven by one dominating passion, are monomaniacs, so to speak, and this ruling passion or monomania can be used to create humorous interactions among the characters.

We are now ready to use the techniques in this glossary to examine Shakespeare's *The Comedy of Errors* and see how he uses these techniques to generate mirthful laughter in his masterful works.

The critics and literary historians of the nineteenth century, that century which saw the inception and progressive development of scholarship as we know it today, were not able to penetrate beyond a surface interpretation of the portrayal of doubles in literature. Having noted it as a technique in comedy, they went on to ascribe its use in prose fiction generally to the predilection of the author for the unreal and uncanny, to his desire to depict distinct and separate traits of himself, or his desire for another existence. [...] It remained for psychoanalysis, with both its clinical and cultural interests, to examine this motif in terms of depth psychology and myth and to relate its use more clearly to the authors themselves. [...] Such examination demonstrated that his use of the double-theme derived not so much from the author's conscious fondness for describing preternatural situations [...] or separate parts of their personalities [...] as from their unconscious impulse to lend imagery to a universal human problem—that of the relation of the self to the self.

Harry Tucker. Introduction to Otto Rank, *The Double: A Psychoanalytic Study*

Chapter 5

THE COMEDY OF ERRORS

The Persons of the Play

SOLINUS, Duke of Ephesus
EGEON, a merchant of Syracuse, father of the Antipholus twins
ANTIPHOLUS OF EPHESUS
ANTIPHOLUS OF SYRACUSE
DROMIO OF EPHESUS
DROMIO OF SYRACUSE
ADRIANA, wife of Antipholus of Syracuse
LUCIANA, her sister
LUCE, Adriana's kitchen maid, also known as NELL
BALTHAZAR, a merchant
ANGELO, a goldsmith
DOCTOR PINCH, a schoolmaster
FIRST MERCHANT, friend to Antipholus of Ephesus
SECOND MERCHANT, to whom Angelo owes a debt
EMILIA, an Abbess at Ephesus
COURTESAN
JAILER
OFFICERS
Headmen, Attendants

Synopsis of *The Comedy of Errors*

Act I

Because a law forbids merchants from Syracuse to enter Ephesus, elderly Syracusian trader Egeon faces execution when he is discovered in the city. He can only escape by paying a fine of a thousand marks. He tells his sad story to Solinus, Duke of Ephesus. In his youth, Egeon married and had twin sons. On the same day, a poor woman without a job also gave birth to twin boys, and he purchased these as slaves to his sons. Soon afterward, the family made a sea voyage and was hit by a tempest. Egeon lashed himself to the main-mast with one son and one slave, and his wife took the other two infants. His wife was rescued by one boat, Egeon by another. Egeon never again saw his wife or the children with her. Recently his son Antipholus, now grown, and his son's slave Dromio left Syracuse to find their brothers. When Antipholus did not return, Egeon set out in search of him. The Duke is moved by this story and grants Egeon one day to pay his fine. That same day, Antipholus arrives in Ephesus, searching for his brother. He sends Dromio to deposit some money at *The Centaur*, an inn. He is confounded when the identical Dromio of Ephesus appears almost immediately, denying any knowledge of the money and asking him home to dinner, where his wife is waiting. Antipholus, thinking his servant is making insubordinate jokes, beats Dromio of Ephesus.

Act II

Dromio of Ephesus returns to his mistress, Adriana, saying that her "husband" refused to come back to his house, and even pretended not to know her. Adriana, concerned that her husband's eye is straying, takes this news as confirmation of her suspicions. Antipholus of Syracuse, who complains "I could not speak with Dromio since at first, I sent him from the mart," meets up with Dromio of Syracuse who now denies making a "joke" about Antipholus having a wife. Antipholus begins beating him. Suddenly, Adriana rushes up to Antipholus of Syracuse and begs him not to leave her. The Syracusans cannot but attribute these strange events to witchcraft, remarking that Ephesus is known as a warren for witches. Antipholus and Dromio go off with this strange woman, the one to eat dinner and the other to keep the gate. Antipholus of Ephesus returns home and is refused entry to his own house.

Act III

Antipholus of Ephesus returns home for dinner and is enraged to find that he is rudely refused entry to his own house by Dromio of Syracuse, who is keeping the gate. He is ready to break down the door, but his friends persuade him not to make a scene. He decides, instead, to dine with a courtesan. Inside the house, Antipholus of Syracuse discovers that he is very attracted to his "wife's" sister, Luciana of Smyrna, telling her "train me not, sweet mermaid, with thy note / To drown me in thy sister's flood of tears." She is flattered by his attention but worried about their moral implications. After she exits, Dromio of Syracuse announces that he has discovered that he has a wife: Nell, a hideous kitchen-maid. He describes her as "spherical, like a globe; I could find out countries in her." Antipholus jokingly asks him to identify the countries, leading to a witty exchange in which parts of her body are identified with nations. Ireland is her buttocks: "I found it out by the bogs."

He claims he has discovered America and the Indies "upon her nose all o'er embellished with rubies, carbuncles, sapphires, declining their rich aspect to the hot breath of Spain; who sent whole armadas of cracks to be ballast at her nose." The Syracusans decide to leave as soon as possible, and Dromio runs off to make travel plans. Antipholus of Syracuse is then confronted by Angelo of Ephesus, a goldsmith, who claims that Antipholus ordered a chain from him. Antipholus is forced to accept the chain, and Angelo says that he will return for payment.

Act IV

Antipholus of Ephesus dispatches Dromio of Ephesus to purchase a rope so that he can beat his wife Adriana for locking him out, then is accosted by Angelo, who tells him "I thought to have ta'en you at the Porpentine" and asks to be reimbursed for the chain. He denies ever seeing it and is promptly arrested. As he is being led away, Dromio of Syracuse arrives, whereupon Antipholus dispatches him back to Adriana's house to get money for his bail. After completing this errand, Dromio of Syracuse mistakenly delivers the money to Antipholus of Syracuse. The Courtesan spies Antipholus wearing the gold chain, and says he promised it to her in exchange for her ring. The Syracusans deny this and flee.

Act V

The Courtesan resolves to tell Adriana that her husband is insane. Dromio of Ephesus returns to the arrested Antipholus of Ephesus, with the rope. Antipholus is infuriated. Adriana, Luciana and the Courtesan enter with a conjurer named Pinch, who tries to exorcise the Ephesians, who are bound and taken to Adriana's house. The Syracusans enter, carrying swords, and everybody runs off for fear: believing that they are the Ephesians, out for vengeance after somehow escaping their bonds. Adriana reappears with henchmen, who attempt to bind the Syracusans. They take sanctuary in a nearby priory, where the Abbess resolutely protects them. Suddenly, the Abbess enters with the Syracusan twins, and everyone begins to understand the confusing events of the day. Not only are the two sets of twins reunited, but the Abbess reveals that she is Egeon's wife, Emilia of Babylon. The Duke pardons Egeon. All exit into the abbey to celebrate the reunification of the family.

https://en.wikipedia.org/wiki/The_Comedy_of_Errors

THE COMEDY OF ERRORS

What is Comedy?

In the introduction to his book, *Comedy*, Andrew Stott defines comedy (2005:1):

> Providing a simple formula to answer the question "what is comedy?" is not so easy. On the one hand, comedy is a reasonably graspable literary form, most properly applied to drama, that uses stock character types in a scenario where some kind of a problem must be resolved. Comedies end happily, often with some kind of communal celebration such as a feast or a marriage. We might add that we would expect a comedy to be funny, and that during the course of its action no one will be killed. But this definition is fine just so long as we understand comedy in its strictest and most restrictive form within literary history.

As Stott points out in his book, there are many other kinds of comedy, but for our purposes, his definition is useful. The problem that has to be resolved in *The Comedy of Errors* involves a search by several members of a family for a missing brother and their mother, who became separated from one another during a storm at sea.

In *The Comedy of Errors*, Shakespeare has two sets of twins, enabling him to play with the comedy of identity to his heart's delight. Much of the comedy in the play comes from mistakes in identity (number 29 in my typology) in which Antipholus of Ephesus interacts with Dromio of Syracuse and Antipholus of Syracuse interacts with Dromio of Ephesus, with comic results. The play is about endless mistakes characters make in interacting with other characters who they assume they know because they look like ones with whom they are familiar. The subtext of the play is the question of identity and the way people both search for a self and the way they interact with others based on their looks. The play is based upon the difference between appearance and reality, with errors—mistakes about people's identities—informing the play.

In her book, *The Cambridge Introduction to Shakespeare's Comedies*, Penny Gay discusses the role the plays of Plautus had on Shakespeare's design of the play (2008:18–19):

> Shakespeare uses, from his source in the Roman playwright Plautus' plays, the unities of place (the street in Ephesus), time (from morning till 5 pm of one day), and action (a single plot logically developed from one situation). Farce still tends to use these conventions (they are familiar from TV sitcoms), complete with mistaken identities, locked-door gags, etc. To Plautus's original play, *The Menaechmi*

with its twin brother protagonists—Antipholus of Syracuse, the visitor, and Antipholus of Ephesus, the local—he adds twin servants, the two Dromios, from another Plautus play, *Amphitruo*. The potential for visual jokes, mistaken identities, and double-takes as people appear from the "wrong part" of the stage is doubled. And so is the potential for laughter and pain.

On the Psychoanalytic Significance of Doubles

The psychoanalytic significance of doubles—in this case, two sets of doubles—is something we might keep in mind as we read the play. In Otto Rank's book, *The Double: A Psychoanalytic Study*, doubles are a much more complicated phenomenon than we imagine and Shakespeare's use of doubles tells us something about his psyche and his study of identity and the search, of his characters, for a self and maybe his search for a self, as well.

Another author with a psychoanalytic perspective, Simon Lesser, offers other insights into the nature of comedy in his book, *Fiction and the Unconscious* (1957:276):

> Comic characters may be indolent, unreliable, vain, hypocritical, frivolous, acquisitive, or lascivious—and sometimes a single character has almost this entire roster of failings. But while such failings may arouse scorn, they do not excite fear. Particularly since they are usually buttressed by such qualities as cunning and resilience, they do not threaten to involve the characters in anything worse than the kind of scrapes from which, after a little squirming, we feel sure they will be able to extricate themselves

Later in the book, Lesser adds more to his discussion of comedy (1957:279):

> It is willing, and even desirous, that every Jack shall have his Jill. But it wants to tease Jack a bit first for our pleasure. It knows that in the end he will prize his Jill more, and we will enjoy their union the more if it is not brought about straightaway. The danger of this course is that we may also have to share the anxiety characters experience during the more discouraging phases of their affairs. To prevent this from happening, comedy nearly always will find some way of letting the reader know that everything will work out in the end. It may make us privy at once to the explanation of difficulties which perplex the characters. Shakespeare employs this device, for example, in *The Comedy of Errors*, and *A Midsummer Night's Dream*.

With these insights in mind, let us examine the perplexed characters in *The Comedy of Errors*.

We learn, at the beginning of the play, about the birth of the two sets of twins. Egeon, the father of the Antipholus twins, describes their birth:

> EGEON
> There she had not been long, but she became
> A joyful mother of two goodly sons.
> And which was strange, the one so like the other
> As could not be distinguished but by names.
> That very hour, in the selfsame inn,
> A mean woman was delivered
> Of such a burden, male twins both alike
> Those, for their parents were exceedingly poor,
> I bought and bought up to attend my sons

Because of a disastrous sea voyage, one son (and his mother) was separated from his father, Egeon explains that he has been searching for him for five years and that his other son took the lost son's name. So we have two sets of identical twin men: two men named Antipholus and two men named Dromio. Because Syracuse doesn't allow people from Ephesus to visit it, on pain of death or a very large fine, the Duke sentences Egeon to death, unless he can find a thousand marks to pay for his life.

> DUKE
> But though thou art adjudged to the death,
> And passed sentence may not be recalled
> But to our honor's great disparagement,
> Yet will I favor thee in what I can.
> Therefore, merchant, I'll limit thee this day
> To see thy help by beneficial health.
> Try all the friends thou hast in Ephesus;
> Beg thou, or borrow, to make up the sum,
> And live. If not, then thou art doomed to die.
> Jailer, take him to thy custody.

It is in the next scene that the comedy begins. It turns out that Antipholus of Syracuse and his servant Dromio have just come to Ephesus. Antipholus of Syracuse sends Dromio to bring the money he had just been given by a merchant to the Centaur and was told to stay there until Antipholus came there.

ANTIPHOLUS OF SYRACUSE
Go bear it to the Centaur, where we host.
And stay there, Dromio, till I come to thee.
Within this hour will be dinnertime.
Till that, I'll view the manner of the town.

Antipholus invites the merchant to dine with him, but the merchant is busy and says he will join him later.

FIRST MERCHANT
Sir, I commend you to your own content.

ANTIPHOLUS OF SYRACUSE
He that commends me to mine own content
Commends me to the thing I cannot get.
I to the world am like a drop of water
That in the ocean seeks another drop,
Who, falling there to find his fellow forth,
Unseen, inquisitive, confounds himself.
So I, to find a mother and a brother,
In quest of them, unhappy, lose myself.

At this point, Dromio of Ephesus appears.

ANTIPHOLUS OF SYRACUSE
Here comes the almanac of my true date?
--What now? How chance thou art returned so soon.

DROMIO OF EPHESUS
Returned so soon? Rather approached too late.
The capon burns, the pig falls from the spit. [...]

After a lengthy speech, Antipholus replies, thinking he is talking to his servant, Dromio.

ANTIPHOLUS OF SYRACUSE
Stop in your wind, sir. Tell me this, I pray.
Where have you left the money that I gave you?

Dromio tells Antipholus that he was sent to fetch him to dinner and that he didn't receive any gold from him. Later we read:

ANTIPHOLUS OF SYRACUSE
Now, as I am a Christian, answer me
In what safe place have you bestowed my money,
Or I shall break that merry sconce of yours,
That stands on tricks when I am undisposed.
Where is the thousand marks thou hadst of me?

Dromio says he received no money from Antipholus and bids him come home to dinner.

ANTIPHOLUS OF SYRACUSE
What, will thou flout me thus unto my face.
Being forbid? There, take that, sir knave!

He strikes Dromio who runs away.

On Comedic Violence

There is a considerable amount of violence in this comedy, as both Dromios are routinely beaten, but not by their masters it turns out, for one reason or another. This is generally because Antipholus of Syracuse is speaking with Dromio of Ephesus and Antipholus of Ephesus is speaking with Dromio of Syracuse and there are countless misunderstandings. In addition, Adriana beat her Dromio.

DROMIO OF EPHESUS
I have some marks of yours upon my pate,
Some of my mistress' marks upon my shoulders,

Violence is generally antithetical to comedy, but we must remember that when people go to comedy, they make certain allowances for the events in the work and see the violence as comedic and not hostile. There is what we might describe as a play frame that tempers our reaction to the violence. There is also the matter of how the actors playing Antipholus strike their servants. I see this violence as a form of slapstick, number 41 in my typology.

Shakespeare uses this device of Antipholus of Syracuse mistaking Dromio of Ephesus for his slave and Antipholus of Ephesus mistaking Dromio of Syracuse for his slave and when the conversations are problematical, each Dromio ends up being beaten by the other Dromio's master. Accepting that this could actually happen requires a considerable suspension of disbelief by the audiences, for it implies that identity is purely physical and based solely on the way characters look. But when we attend a comedy, there is a relaxation of our critical faculties in the service of hoped-for pleasure. When the play is produced, the characters playing the male leads also don't really look alike, though they are dressed alike, so audiences are willing to play along with the game.

The scene changes to one with Adriana, wife of Antipholus of Ephesus, and her sister, Luciana. Adriana is complaining that neither her husband nor his slave has returned. This leads to a discussion of the relationship that exists between men and women and husbands and wives.

LUCIANA
Man, more divine, the master of all these,
Lord of the wide world and wild wat'ry seas,
Indued with intellectual sense and souls,
Of more preeminence than fish and fowls,
Are masters to their females, and their lords:
Then let you will attend on their accords.
ADRIANA
This servitude makes you to keep unwed.
ADRIANA
Not this, but troubles of the marriage bed.
ADRIANA
But were you wedded, you would bear some sway.
LUCIANA
Ere I learn love, I'll practice to obey.

This conversation tells us a good deal about Shakespeare's ideas about how husbands and wives relate to one another. Luciana is "conservative" in that she seems to believe that the duty of the wife is to "obey," and that husbands must be "masters to their females." Adriana, who is married, has other ideas and says that were Luciana wedded, she would behave differently.

They continue their conversation when Dromio of Ephesus returns saying his conversation with Antipholus (of Syracuse) showed he was crazy, or "horn mad."

DROMIO OF EPHESUS
I mean not cuckold mad,
But he is stark mad.
When I desired him to come home for dinner,
He asked me for a thousand marks in gold.
'Tis dinner time," quoth I. "My gold!" quoth he.

"Your meat doth burn," quoth I. "My gold!" quoth he.
"Where is the thousand marks I gave thee, villain?"
"The pig, quoth I, "is burned. "My gold!" quoth he.
"My mistress, sir—"quote I. "Hang up thy mistress."
"I know," quoth he, "no house, no wife, no mistress."

Dromio adds that Antipholus beat him. Adriana tells Dromio to go back and fetch her husband but Dromio refuses, telling her to send some other messenger. The scene ends with Adriana very upset and afraid that her husband has found another love.

In the next scene, we have another encounter based on mistaken identities—between Antipholus of Syracuse and Dromio of Ephesus. The two mechanisms operating here are technique 21, ignorance, and technique 29, mistakes. There may also be an element of technique 35, reversal, and technique 44, theme and variation. The Ephesus/Syracuse relationship is reversed and we have a Syracuse/Ephesus relationship, which is why I think reversal is an aspect of the comedy here.

In this scene, Adriana and Luciana encounter them.

ADRIANA
How comes it now, my husband, oh, how comes it,
That thou art estranged from thyself?
Thy "self" I call it, being stranged to me
That, undividable incorporate,
Am better than thy dear self's better part.
ANTIPHOLUS OF SYRACUSE
Plead you to me, fair dame? I know you not.
In Ephesus I am but two hours old.
As strange as to your town as to your talk.

This speech by Adriana deals with the central question of the play: what is the "self" and how do people become estranged from others and their "selves"? The play revolves around mistaken identities and the role that personal appearances play in conferring an identity upon someone. The characters in the play from Ephesus cannot conceive of (or are not allowed to conceive of) there being a twin brother of the Antipholus and another twin brother of the Dromio they know and so pay no attention when, for example, Antipholus of Syracuse tells Adriana he's only been in Syracuse for two hours. In a sense, *The Comedy of Errors* is about the way people search for an identity and a self and the way people can become deluded by appearances in dealing with their identities and the identities of others.

Dromio of Syracuse adds that he has never seen Adriana before, which is correct because Adriana has interacted with Dromio of Ephesus. Luciana tells Dromio to go to the servants and have them prepare dinner. Dromio talks to himself about being confronted with goblins and sprites, to which Luciana says:

LUCIANA
Why prat'st though to thyself and answer not.
Dromio, thou drone, thou snail, thou slug, thou sot!

Here we have comedic insult, technique 25. As with violence, in the play frame that seeing a comedy requires, we recognize that the insults are not serious but essentially a means of injecting another kind of humor into a conversation. I would classify this comedic violence as a form of slapstick (technique 41). There are several places where insults are used for comic effects, such as in the shouting match between the two Dromios. We also find coincidence (technique 11) has an important role in the play.

Adriana and Luciana convince Antipholus and Dromio to come to dinner and tell Dromio to guard the gate, setting up a scene in which Adriana's husband comes home with his Dromio and finds the gate to his house locked. This sets up a shouting match between the two Dromios.

DROMIO OF EPHESUS (calling)
Maud, Bridget, Marian, Cicely, Gillian, Ginn!
[Enter Dromio of Syracuse, within]

DROMIO OF SYRACUSE
Mome, Malt-horse, Capon, Coxcomb, Idio, Patch!
Either get thee from the door, or sit down at the hatch.
Dost thou conjure for wenches, that thou cal'st for such store
When one is one too many? Go, get thee from the door.

Members of the audience are asked to assume that the two Dromios, twin brothers, would not recognize each other's voices. Antipholus of Syracuse decides to get a crowbar to break down the door but is persuaded to leave by Balthasar and go to dinner at a restaurant. Antipholus agrees and decides they will go to dine with a courtesan he knows.

The scene shifts to a conversation between Antipholus of Syracuse, who Luciana thinks is Adrian's husband, and Luciana. Luciana tells him to comfort her sister, Adriana. Antipholus replies.

ANTIPHOLUS OF SYRACUSE
Sweet mistress, what your name is else I know not.

Nor by what wonder you do hit of mine [...]
Your weeping sister is no wife of mine,
Nor to her bed no homage do I owe.
Far more, far more, to you do I decline.
Oh, train me not, sweet mermaid, with thy note
To drown me in thy sister's flood of tears.
Sing, siren, for thyself, and I will dote.
Spread o'er the silver waves thy golden hairs,
And as a bed I'll take thee, and there lie,
And in that glorious supposition think:
He gains by death that hath such means to die.
Let love, being light, be drowned if she sink.

He adds later:

ANTIPHOLUS OF SYRACUSE
Thee will I love, and with thee lead my life.
Thou hast no husband yet, nor I a wife.
Give me thy hand.

Luciana pays no attention to what Antipholus of Syracuse tells her because she thinks she knows Antipholus and has confidence in what she believes and knows rather than in taking seriously what Antipholus has to say. In addition, what Antipholus of Syracuse says about not being married to Adriana seems to her to be quite preposterous. To this, we must add the astonishment at being told that he, her sister's husband (so she believes), is in love with her.

Antipholus sees Dromio who informs him that he also has found a woman to be his wife, which leads to a long conversation about her in which Dromio says he can find many countries in the woman, Nell, who is Adrian's kitchen-maid, Luce.

ANTIPHOLUS OF SYRACUSE
In what part of her body stands Ireland?
DROMIO OF SYRACUSE
Marry, sir, in her buttocks. I found it out by the bogs.
ANTIPHOLUS OF SYRACUSE
Where Scotland?
DROMIO OF SYRACUSE
I found it by the barrenness, hard in the palm of her hand.
ANTIPHOLUS OF SYRACUSE
Where France?

DROMIO OF SYRACUSE
In her forehead, armed and reverted, making war with her hair.

This passage, and I've not quoted all of the dialogue, is an example of stereotyping (Technique 43), which is a commonly used technique by humorists—playing upon commonly held and inaccurate ideas people have about what people in other countries are like. When we stereotype people, generally we are putting them down, which suggests there is an element of superiority in this kind of humor. That is, when we stereotype people, we feel superior to them and this superiority was, for Aristotle, the basis of comedy.

So, as the result of Antipholus going to dinner at Adriana's house, both he and Dromio have found women who will be their wives. There is a logical problem here. Antipholus of Syracuse asks Luciana what her name is, which ordinarily would cause her to wonder why he doesn't know her name. And he wonders how people in Syracuse know his name. He has told Adriana that he's only been in Syracuse for two hours, but she pays no attention to that information. Adriana, Luciana and others, discount information provided by Antipholus of Syracuse because they believe they know him and have known him for many years.

The Madness Scene

It is the madness scene, with the crank Dr. Pinch, that leads to the resolution of the comedy.

The Courtesan encounters Antipholus of Syracuse and invites him to dine with her again. They think she is a sorceress.

COURTESAN
Give me the ring of mine you had at dinner,
Or for my diamond the chain you promised.
And I'll be gone, sire, and not trouble you....
ANTIPHOLUS OF SYRACUSE
Avaunt, thou witch!—Comes, Dromio, let us go.

They leave.

COURTESAN
Now out of doubt, Antipholus is mad,
Else he would never so demean himself.
A ring he hath of mine worth forty ducats,
Both one and other he denies me now.

The reason that I gather he is mad,
Besides the present instance of his rage,
Is a mad tale he told me today at dinner
Of his own doors being shut against his entrance.
Belike his wife, acquainted with his fits,
On purpose shut the doors against his way.

Antipholus of Syracuse enters with an officer. Dromio enters with a rope. Antipholus asks him for his ducats, and Dromio replies that he gave the money for a rope. Antipholus gets angry and beats Dromio again. At this point, Adriana, Luciana, the Courtesan and the schoolmaster, Pinch, enter.

COURTESAN
How say you now? Is not your husband mad?
ADRIANA
His incivility confirms no less.
--Good Doctor Pinch, you are a conjurer.
Establish him in his true sense again.
And I will please you.
PINCH TO ANTIPHOLUS OF EPHESUS
Give me your hand and let me feel your pulse.
ANTIPHOLUS
There is my hand, and let it feel your ear.
[He strikes Pinch.]
PINCH
I charge thee, Satan, housed within this man,
To yield possession to my holy prayers,
And to thy state of darkness hie the straight
I conjure thee by all the saints in heaven.

This leads to a confrontation between Antipholus of Ephesus and his wife, in which Antipholus argues about whether he dined at home. Adriana insists he dined with her, not realizing she dined with his twin brother, and Dromio of Syracuse, insists that the door was locked and he dined elsewhere.

PINCH
Mistress, both man and master is possessed:
I know by their pale and deadly looks.
They must be bound and laid in some dark room.

The officers bind Antipholus and Dromio and Adriana tells them to bring them to her house.

They take Antipholus and Dromio off, while the officer, Adriana, Luciana and the Courtesan remain.

It is worth noting that sending Antipholus and Dromio to a dark room is like what happened to Malvolio in *Twelfth Night*. He, too, was judged "mad" and sent to a dark room to recover. Madness plays a role in both comedies and, in both cases, the diagnosis is incorrect. Shortly after Antipholus of Ephesus and his slave Dromio are taken away by the officers, Antipholus of Syracuse and his slave Dromio enter, with their rapiers drawn.

> LUCIANA
> God, for thy mercy, they are loose again!
> ADRIANA
> And come with naked swords; let's call for more help.
> To have them bound again.
> OFFICER
> Away, they'll kill us.
> [Exeunt all, as fast as may be, frighted.]

Antipholus then tells Dromio to get their stuff from the Centaur so they can take a boat that is leaving that evening.

In the next scene, two merchants and the goldsmith, Angelo, are talking when Antipholus of Syracuse and his slave Dromio enter.

> ANGELO
> This chain you had of me. Can you deny it?
> ANTIPHOLUS OF SYRACUSE.
> I think I had. I never did deny it.
> SECOND MERCHANT
> These ears of mine thou know'st did hear thee.
> Fie on thee, wretch! 'Tis a pity thou liv'st.
> To talk where any honest men resort.

They are about to fight when Adriana, Luciana, the Courtesan and others appear.

> ADRIANA
> Hold, hurt him not, for God's sake! He is mad.
> Some get within him, take his sword away.
> Bind Dromio too, and bear them to my house.

Antipholus of Syracuse and his slave Dromio then run away and take shelter in a priory. The stage is set now for the resolution of the play when Antipholus of Syracuse encounters his brother Antipholus of Ephesus and their twin slaves Dromio of Syracuse and Dromio of Ephesus meet, encounter their father and discover the prioress is their long-lost mother.

This resolution is described by Penny Gay in her book *The Cambridge Introduction to Shakespeare's Comedies* (2008:21):

> Here, Shakespeare, the true magician, pulls another rabbit out of the hat: the moment when both sets of twins see each other for the first time. It's what the audience has been waiting for and expecting—so the basic dramatic value suspense is invoked—but it is much more than that. It is in fact magic—the magic of stagecraft, in which two sets of actors, and their costume and make-up designers, have used all their techniques to convince us that they are identical. [...]The writing for both sets of twins goes beyond the simple comic resolution of the farcical errors: Shakespeare calls up some profoundly beautiful poetry to move as well as delight us with the mystery of human identity and the strange but strong bonds of familiar relationships.

Gay's point is that resolving the play is more than a matter of wrapping up loose points and is, in fact, a profound comment on the mystery of human identity.

In narratives of all kinds, there is often a scene in which everything is resolved. For example, in murder mysteries, it is common for the detective to summon all the suspects together, describe his or her thinking in solving the mystery and say who committed the murder. In comedies, there is usually a resolution in which everything that was confusing is explained, followed by a celebration or a wedding.

The Resolution of *The Comedy of Errors*

The resolution of *The Comedy of Errors* takes place in the priory, where Antipholus of Syracuse and his slave Dromio have taken refuge. Adriana tells the prioress she wants to bring him home, but the prioress refuses.

> ABBESS
> He took this place for sanctuary,
> And it shall privilege him from your hands
> Till I have brought him to his wits again,
> Or lose my labor in assaying it.

The Duke of Ephesus, Egeon, two merchants and other officers arrive at the scene.

DUKE
Yet once again proclaim it publicly
If any friend will not pay the sum for him,
He shall not die; so much we tender him.

Adriana tells the Duke about her husband and Dromio's behavior, describing them both as mad. The Duke commands the abbess to be brought before him when a messenger arrives.

MESSENGER
0 mistress, mistress, shift and save yourself.
My master and his man are both broke loose,
Beaten the maids a-row, and bound the Doctor,
Whose beard they have singed off with brands of fire,
And ever as it blazed, they threw on him
Great pails of puddled mire to quench the hair.

ADRIANA
Peace, fool, thy master and his man are here
And that is false thou dost report to us.

There is a cry within that is heard. The Duke tells Adriana not to worry. Then Antipholus of Ephesus and his slave Dromio appear.

ANTIPHOLUS OF EPHESUS
Justice, most gracious Duke, oh, grant me justice.
Even for the service that long since I did thee,
When I bestrid thee in the wars and took
Deep scars to save thy life; even for the blood
That then I lost for thee, now grant me justice.
EGEON [aside]
Unless the fear of death doth make me dote,
I see my son Antipholus and Dromio.

This is followed by a long discussion in which Angelo the goldsmith says that he was with Antipholus when he was locked out of his house. After this discussion, Egeon speaks to the Duke.

EGEON
Most mighty Duke, vouchsafe me speak a word.

> Haply I see a friend will save my life
> And pay the sum that may deliver me.
> DUKE
> Speak freely, Syracusan, what thou wilt.
> EGEON [to Antipholus of Ephesus]
> Is not your name, sir, called Antipholus?
> And is not that bondman Dromio?

He adds that he's sure they both remember him, but Antipholus of Ephesus replies that he's never seen him before.

> EGEON
> Tell me, art thou my son Antipholus?
> ANTIPHOLUS OF SYRACUSE
> I never saw my father in my life.

Antipholus protests he does not know Egeon when the Abbess enters with Antipholus of Syracuse and Dromio of Syracuse. This is the critical moment of the play when the two sons of Egeon and the two Dromios confront one another.

> ADRIANA
> I see two husbands, or mine eyes deceive me.
> DUKE
> One of these men is genius to the other,
> And so, of these, which is the natural man,
> And which the spirit? Who deciphers them?
> DROMIO OF SYRACUSE
> I, sir, am Dromio. Command him away.
> DROMIO OF EPHESUS
> I, sir, am Dromio. Let me stay.
> ANTIPHOLUS OF SYRACUSE
> Egeon, art thou not? Or else his ghost.
> DROMIO OF SYRACUSE
> O my old master! Who hath bound him here?

This is followed by a speech by the abbess that resolves everything.

> ABBESS
> Whoever bound him, I will loose his bonds
> And gain a husband by his liberty.

Speak, old Egeon, if thou beest the man
That had a wife once called Emilia,
That bore thee at a burden two fair sons.
Of, if thou beest the same Egeon, speak,
And speak unto the same Emilia.

The two brothers describe what happened in Ephesus and we learn how there were many errors in how the money changed hands that now can be understood. Antipholus of Syracuse offers to pay for his father's life, but the Duke says he doesn't want the money. The final speech of the abbess resolves everything.

ABBESS
Renowned Duke, vouchsafe to take the pains
To go with us into the abbey here,
And hear at large all our fortunes.
And all that are assembled in this place,
That by this sympathized one day's error
Have suffered wrong, go, keep us company
And we shall make full satisfaction.
Thirty-three years have I but gone in travail
Of you, my sons, and till the present hour
My heavy burden ne'er delivered.
The Duke, my husband, and my children both,
And you the calendars of their nativity,
Go to gossip's feast and go with me—
After so much grief such nativity.
DUKE
With all my heart, I'll gossip at this feast.

The two Dromios, not being sure who is the older one, decide to go to the feast hand in hand,
    And with that, the play ends—as comedies should end, with a feast celebrating the two brothers having found one another and their father having found his long-lost wife, and with Antipholus of Syracuse having the prospect of marrying Luciana.

Basic Humorous Techniques in *The Comedy of Errors*

We find the following techniques from my typology, some of which, such as mistakes, are used frequently:

Number 29: Mistakes, errors.
The title of the play tells us that this will be the dominant means of generating humor in the play and it is full of errors as one character after another mistakes one of the brothers for the other.

Number 11: Coincidences
Many of the mistakes in the plot are based upon coincidences in which Dromio from Ephesus comes into contact with Antipholus of Syracuse or vice versa (reversal, technique number 35) and they don't realize with whom they are talking.

Number 25: Insults
There are several scenes in which one character insults another. Usually, the recipient of these insults is one of the two Dromios. For example, Adriana calls Dromio a drone, a snail, a slug and a sot. And later, an ass.

> LUCIANA
> Why prat'st though to thyself and answer not.
> Dromio, thou drone, thou snail, thou slug, thou sot.

Number 41: Slapstick
I define comic violence as a form of physical humor called slapstick. I point out that the violence, which occurs frequently in the play, isn't upsetting because the audience is watching the play recognizing that it isn't real. I would also classify the way Dr. Pinch is treated as comic violence and slapstick.

> My master and his man are both broke loose,
> Beaten the maids a-row, and bound the Doctor,
> Whose beard they have singed off with brands of fire,
> And ever as it blazed, they threw on him
> Great pails of puddled mire to quench the hair.

This treatment of Dr. Pinch is a subject of considerable interest by Shakespeare scholars, some of whom think it, and the violence, is of central importance in the play.

Number 10: Chase scene
This refers to the last part of the play in which characters are racing around, finally ending up in the abbey where the twin brothers encounter one another, their father and their mother. This enables everyone to understand, finally, why there has been such confusion that day.

Number 35: Reversal
Here I am alluding to the way each of the Antipholus brothers, without realizing what he is doing, beats his brother's slave. Thus, Antipholus of Syracuse beats Dromio of Ephesus, and Antipholus of Ephesus beats Dromio of Syracuse.

Number 42: Stereotyping
We find this in the scene in which the national character of people from different countries is discussed and we learn about what the French, the Scots and so on are like. Dromio is talking about Nell and says there are many countries in her body.

> ANTIPHOLUS OF SYRACUSE
> In what part of her body stands Ireland?
> DROMIO OF SYRACUSE
> Marry, sir, in her buttocks. I found it out by the bogs.
> ANTIPHOLUS OF SYRACUSE
> Where Scotland?
> DROMIO OF SYRACUSE
> I found it by the barrenness, hard in the palm of her hand.

Humor writers count on the stereotypes people have about people from other countries to create humor, often in the form of weak or strong insults and invidious comparisons.

A Paradigmatic Analysis of *The Comedy of Errors*

In my chapter on the semiotics of comedy, I discuss the work of Claude Lévi-Strauss, who suggested that the paradigmatic analysis of a text, its bipolar oppositions, tells us what it is about, and provides us with its latent or unrecognized but important content. Let me suggest the following set of binary oppositions can be found in the play.

Appearance	Reality
Separation	Connection
Loss	Recovery
Error	Correction
Twins	Singletons
Similarities	Differences
Sisters	Brothers
Fathers	Sons

Husbands	Wives
Wives	Courtesans
Strangers	Natives
Royalty	Commoners
Quests	Satisfactions
Madness	Sanity
Single	Married
Life	Death

Because of the nature of language, our minds work to find oppositions to give things meaning. Recall that Saussure pointed out that concepts have no meaning in themselves but take their meaning through oppositions: rich/poor, happy/sad/ healthy/sick, lost/found. So, when we watch a play like *The Comedy of Errors*, our minds are continually, but unconsciously, making the binary oppositions to give what is said and done meaning.

A Syntagmatic Analysis of *The Comedy of Errors*

Here we apply, in simplified form, the linear sequence of elements or functions in the text. That is, we examine what the characters do, how their activities relate to one another and affect one another, and the story as a whole. In his *Morphology of the Folktale*, Propp argued that a function can be understood to be (1928/1968:21) "an act of a character, defined from the point of view of its significance for the course of action." He argues that all tales begin with an initial situation in which the members of a family or a hero are introduced and that this initial situation is not a function. Some functions in folktales, in modified and simplified form, that we find in *The Comedy of Errors* follow. They are all found in Propp's chapter on "The Functions of Dramatis Personae."

Initial situation.
We are introduced to Egeon and the Duke.

One of the members of a family absents himself from home.
We find this with the storm in which the members of the family become separated from one another in the storm.

An interdiction is violated.
Egeon is told by the Duke that people from Syracuse are not allowed in Ephesus and that if he can't pay a fine by that evening, he will be killed.

One member of a family lacks something or desires something.
Egeon of Syracuse is searching for his lost son, and his son Antipholus of Syracuse is searching for his lost brother.

The hero is led to the whereabouts of an object of his search. Also: The hero, unrecognized, arrives in a different country.
Antipholus arrives in Ephesus, but people in Ephesus do not realize he is not Antipholus of Ephesus because the brothers are identical twins.

The task is resolved.
Egeon finds his lost son, Antipholus of Ephesus, and Antipholus of Syracuse finds his twin brother, Antipholus of Ephesus, and his mother.

The Villain is punished.
Doctor Pinch, the schoolmaster, has his beard singed off.

The hero is recognized.
The abbess recognizes her husband and Egeon is recognized by his twin sons.

The hero is married.
Antipholus of Syracuse will marry Luciana, the sister of his brother's wife, and Dromio of Syracuse will marry Nell.

If you read Propp's book, you find that some of the functions have many possible variations, so what I have provided here is a skeleton of a Proppian analysis of the play, but you can see that many of his functions can be applied to *The Comedy of Errors*, which suggests that there are many folkloristic elements in the play.

In Stephen Greenblatt's introduction to the play, found in *The Norton Shakespeare Comedies*, 3rd edition, we read (2016:269):

> Through a breathless succession of zany doublings and confusions, Shakespeare's comedy discloses the hidden strangeness of ordinary existence. An invitation to dinner, a simple transaction with a goldsmith, the operation of commercial and civil laws, the relationship between master and servant, the bond between husband and wife (or mistress and sister-in-law)—all become unhinged, as if by sorcery.

Greenblatt captures, in this short passage, the genius of *The Comedy of Errors*, one of the most remarkable comedies written by Shakespeare and a brilliant achievement. He points out that in Shakespeare's hands, simple aspects of everyday life become extremely complicated and hilarious. We also have to consider the role that actors and actresses play when *The Comedy of Errors* is reproduced, for performers can turn a play into a magical and memorable experience.

Laughter liberates not only from external censorship but first of all from the great interior censor; it liberates from the fear that has developed in man during thousands of years: fear of the sacred, of prohibitions, of power. It unveils the material bodily principle in its true meaning. Laughter opened men's eyes on that which is new, on the future. This is why it not only permitted the expression of an antifeudal, popular truth; it helped uncover this truth and give it an internal form. And this form was achieved and defended during thousands of years in its very depths and in its popular-festive images. Laughter showed the world anew in its gayest and most sober aspects. Its external privileges are intimately linked with interior forces; they are a recognition of the rights of these forces. This is why laughter could never become an instrument to oppress and blind the people. It always remained a free weapon in their hands.

As opposed to laughter, medieval seriousness was infused with elements of fear, weakness, humility, submission, falsehood, hypocrisy, or on the other hand with violence, intimidation, threats, prohibitions. As a spokesman of power, seriousness terrorized, demanded, and forbade [...] Distrust of the serious tone and confidence in the truth of laughter had a spontaneous, elemental character. It was understood that fear never lurks behind laughter [...] and that hypocrisy and lies never laugh but wear a serious mask. Laughter created no dogmas and could not become authoritarian; it did not convey fear but a feeling of strength. It was linked with the procreating act, with birth, renewal, fertility, abundance. Laughter was also related to food and drink and the people's earthy immortality, and finally, it was related to the future of things to come and was to clear the way for them.

Mikhail Bakhtin, *Rabelais and His World*: 1984:94–5

Chapter 6

CODA

When I decided to write a book on Shakespeare's comedies, I did not know how I would proceed. I love Shakespeare's comedies but I soon realized that I would either have to write an enormous book with chapters on each of his 13 (by some critics) comedies or find a different way to organize my book.

I had written an analysis of *Twelfth Night* that I used in my book, *The Art of Comedy Writing* and that made me think about twins. That led me to write a chapter on *The Comedy of Errors*, which has two sets of identical twins in it, and I concluded that a book about Shakespeare's comedies and one with two sets of identical twins was a good play to analyze in the book.

I decided to offer a chapter on different theories of humor and one on the semiotics of humor for those not familiar with academic discourse on these topics. I also considerably revised a list of techniques of humor that I had developed and written about in several of my books on humor, and that is found in my glossary chapter. I changed many of the examples of the techniques and substituted jokes and other texts for what I used in the original version. I've always felt that a book on humor should have lots of jokes and other kinds of humorous texts in it.

The Importance of Twins

Writing about plays is difficult because I believe it is important to quote relevant lines from the play to illustrate whatever topic I was writing about, which means I had to copy many lines of dialogue. This was a particularly difficult problem with *The Comedy of Errors* because in many cases I had to identify Antipholus of Syracuse or Antipholus of Ephesus and Dromio of Syracuse and Dromio of Ephesus, which resulted in my adopting a different format for this chapter, with the title of the speaker above the dialogue, so readers can know which Antipholus or Dromio Shakespeare was writing about.

Semiotics and Comedy

My analysis of the play is semiotically informed. We see this in my syntagmatic and paradigmatic analyses of *The Comedy of Errors* and in my discussion of some of the techniques of humor—some 45 that I've identified—that Shakespeare employed in writing the play. I had to expand my way of understanding some of my techniques slightly in places. For example, I don't have "disguise" as a technique but it is covered, I think, by Technique 23, Impersonation, and I don't have comic violence listed but believe it can be seen as part of slapstick. There is a considerable amount of violence in *The Comedy of Errors* which is mitigated, perhaps, by the play frame in which people engage when they see a comedy or read a comedy. In slapstick comedy films, there is often a great deal of violence but it is light-hearted and seen as comic rather than vicious and hostile.

If you are interested in humor, and are curious about how comedic texts achieve their ends—mirthful laughter—you can try using the techniques found in my glossary to interpret and analyze Shakespeare's comedies or other humorous texts. Whatever the case, I hope you've enjoyed some of the jokes and other humorous texts in the glossary and you have found this book interesting and learned something both about humor and about how Shakespeare created his magnificent plays.

Arthur

Arthur Asa Berger
Mill Valley, California

REFERENCES

Affective Disposition Theory. https://en.wikipedia.org/wiki/Affective_disposition_theory
Akhtar, S. 2009. "Twinning Quote," in *A Comprehensive Dictionary of Psychoanalysis*, p. 297.
Allen, Woody. 1978. "Spring Bulletin," in *Getting Even*, p. 42. New York: Vantage Books.
Attardo, Salvatore. 2020. "Semiotics of Humor," Published to Oxford Scholarship Online: September 2020. DOI: 10.1093/oso/9780198791270.001.0001
Attardo, Salvatore and Jean-Charles Chabanne. 1992. "Jokes as Text Types," in *Humor*, pp. 165–176.
Bakhtin, Mikhail. 1984. *Rabelais and His World*. Bloomington, IN: Indiana University Press.
Bateson, Gregory. https://www.coursehero.com/file/75061754/Bateson-1952-1pdf/
Beckett, Samuel. 2009. *Krapp's Last Tape*. London: Faber and Faber.
Berger, Arthur Asa. 1970. *Li'l Abner: A Study of American Humor*. New York: Twayne.
Chandler, Daniel. 2002. *Semiotics: The Basics*. London: Routledge.
Douglas, Mary. 1997. "Jokes," in *Implicit Meanings: Essays in Anthropology*, 17–18. London: Routledge and Kegan Paul.
Dryden, John. "Aurang Zebe." https://poets.org/poem/aureng-zebe-prologue
Dundes, Alan. 1928/1968. "Introduction," in Vladimir Propp (Ed.), *Morphology of the Folktale*, xi–xii. Austin, TX: University of Texas Press.
Dynel, Marta. "Humorous Phenomena in Dramatic Discourse." *European Journal of Humor Research* I (1): 22–60.
Fitzgerald, F. Scott. 1925. *The Great Gatsby*. New York: Charles Scribner's Sons.
Freud, Sigmund. 1960. *Jokes and Their Relation to the Unconscious*. New York: W.W. Norton
Fry, William. 1963. *Sweet Madness: A Study of Humor*. Palo Alto, CA: Pacific Books.
Frye, Northrop. 1971. *Anatomy of Criticism: Four Essay*. Princeton, NJ: Princeton University Press.
Gay, Penny. 2008. *The Cambridge Introduction to Shakespeare's Comedies*. Cambridge: Cambridge University Press.
Greenblatt, Stephen, et al. 2016. *The Norton Shakespeare: Comedies*. 3rd ed. New York: W.W.Norton.
Griffiths, Trevor. 1976. *Comedians*. New York: Grove Press.
Hobbes, Thomas. 1957. *Leviathan*. Oxford: Basil Blackwell.
Ionesco, Eugene. 1958. *Four Plays*. New York: Grove Press.
Johnson, Benjamin. 1994. *Volpone*. New York: Dover.
Kant, Immanuel. "Laughter," quoted in Piddington, Ralph. 1963. New York: Gamut Press.

Lakoff, George and Mark Johnson. 1980. *Metaphors We Live By*. Chicago, IL: University of Chicago Press.
Lesser, Simon. 1957. *Fiction and the Unconscious*. Boston, MA: Beacon Press.
McGraw, A. Peter, et al. February 2015. "Humorous Complaining." *Journal of Consumer Research* 41(5): 1153–1171. Published by: Oxford University Press.
Nilsen. Review of Arthur Asa Berger. 1999. *"The Art of Comedy Writing." Journal of Humor Research (Humor)* 12–1: 96, 97.
Piddington, Ralph. 1963. *The Psychology of Laughter*. New York: Gamut Press.
Propp, Vladimir. 1928/1968. *Morphology of the folktale*. Austin, TX: University of Texas Press.
Saussure, Ferdinand de. 1915/1966. *Course in General Linguistics*. New York: McGraw-Hill.
Schopenhauer, Arthur. 1971. "Incongruity Theory," quoted in Piddington, Ralph, *The Psychology of Laughter*.
Shakespeare, William. 2009. *Henry IV Part I*. New York: Modern Library Classics.
Shakespeare, William. 2016. *The Comedy of Errors*. See Greenblatt, Stephen, *The Norton Shakespeare: Comedies*.
Shakespeare, William. 2016. *Twelfth Night*. See Greenblatt, Stephen, *The Norton Shakespeare: Comedies*.
Sheridan, Richard Brinsley. 2008. *The School for Scandal*. Oxford: Oxford University Press.
Simon, Neil. 1971. *The Comedy of Neil Simon*. New York: Avon.
Stoppard, Tom. 1975. *Travesties*. New York: Grove Press.
Stott, Andrew. 2005. *Comedy*. New York: Routledge.
Tucker, Harry. 1874/1979. "Introduction" to Otto Rank, in *The Double: A Psychoanalytic Study*. New York: Meridian.
Wilde, Oscar. 2008. *The Importance of Being Earnest*. New York: Dover.

ABOUT THE AUTHOR

Arthur Asa Berger is Professor Emeritus of Broadcast and Electronic Communication Arts at San Francisco State University, where he taught between 1965 and 2003. He graduated in 1954 from the University of Massachusetts, where he majored in literature and philosophy.

He received an MA degree in journalism and creative writing from the University of Iowa in 1956. He was drafted shortly after graduating from Iowa and served in the U.S. Army in the Military District of Washington in Washington DC, where he was a feature writer and speechwriter in the District's Public Information Office. He also wrote about high school sports for the *Washington Post* on weekend evenings while in the army.

Berger spent a year touring Europe after he got out of the army and then went to the University of Minnesota, where he received a PhD in American Studies in 1965. He wrote his dissertation on the comic strip, *Li'l Abner*. In 1963–64, he had a Fulbright to Italy and taught at the University of Milan.

He spent a year as a visiting professor at the Annenberg School for Communication at The University of Southern California in Los Angeles in 1984 and two months in the fall of 2007 as a visiting professor at the School of Hotel and Tourism in Hong Kong Polytechnic University. He spent a month lecturing at Jinan University in Guangzhou and 10 days lecturing at Tsinghua University in Beijing in Spring 2009. He spent a month in 2012 as a Fulbright Senior Specialist in Argentina, lecturing on semiotics and cultural criticism, a month in Minsk in 2014, and three weeks lecturing on semiotics and media in Iran in 2015. He is the author of over one hundred articles and more than eighty books on semiotics, media, popular culture, humor and tourism.

Berger is married, has two children and four grandchildren and lives in Mill Valley, California. He enjoys foreign travel and classical music. He can be reached by e-mail at arthurasaberger@gmail.com.

INDEX

Akhtar, Salman 8
Allen, Woody 2, 45, 51
Anatomy of Criticism (Frye) 56, 57
An Anatomy of Humor (Berger) 2
Aristotle 5, 6, 12, 53, 77
Art of Comedy Writing (Berger) 2
Attardo, Salvatore 14, 22
Aurang Zebe (Dryden) 35

Bakhtin, Mikhail 88
Bald Soprano (Ionesco) 2, 32, 47
Bateson, Gregory 5, 9, 10
Beckett, Samuel 40, 41
Benny, Jack 2, 52
Bergson, Henri 5, 48
Blind Men and Elephants (Berger) 2
Brooks, Mel 2
Browne, Sir Thomas 35
Bruce, Lenny 2
Bulgakov, Mikhail 43

Caesar, Sid 2
Cambridge Introduction to Shakespeare's Comedies 68, 80
Cantor, J. 10, 11
Capp, Al 1, 55, 56
Cervantes 5
Chabanne, Jean-Charles 22
Chandler, Daniel 20, 21
Come Blow Your Horn (Simon) 39, 41
Comedian (Griffiths) 57
Comedy 68
Comedy (Stott) 68
Comedy of Errors (Shakespeare) 3, 62, 69, 70, 80, 88–90; paradigmatic analysis of 85–86; syntagmatic analysis of 86–87
Comic-Stripped American (Berger) 1
Cops 37

Dangerfield, Rodney 2
Darwin, Charles 15

Double: A Psychoanalytic Study (Rank) 64
Douglas, Mary 4
Dryden, John 25
Duncan, Isadora 52
Dundes, Alan 27
Dynel, Marta 10

Einstein, Albert 15

Fiction and the Unconscious (Lesser) 69
Fitzgerald, F. Scott 36
Franklin, Benjamin 34
Frasier 49
Freud, Sigmund 4, 5, 8, 15
Fry, William 9
Frye, Northrop 56, 57

Gay, Penny 68, 80
Genius of the Jewish Joke (Berger) 2
Great Gatsby (Fitzgerald) 36
Greenblatt, Stephen 87
Griffiths, Trevor 57

Henry IV Part 1 (Shakespeare) 38, 49
Hobbes, Thomas 6, 7
Humor (academic journal) 22; glossary of 45 techniques of 29–59; tables of 45 techniques 29, 30
Humor, Psyche and Society (Berger) 2
Humor and Society: Resistance and Control (Powell and Paton) 7
"Humorous Complaining" 11
"Humorous Phenomena in Dramatic Discourse" x
humorous stock characters: boasters or alazons 61; fools or schlemiels 62; gulls 61; hicks or agroikos 61; old men or senexes 62; pedants 62; pretenders of eirons 61
humorous techniques in *The Comedy of Errors* (Shakespeare): number 10: chase

scene 84; number 11: coincidences 84; number 25: insults 84; number 29: mistakes, errors 84; number 35: reversal 85; number 41: slapstick 84; number 42: stereotyping 85

Implicit Meanings: Essays in Anthropology 4
Importance of Being Earnest 53, 54
"Introduction to Psychology" 51

Jakobson, Roman 20
Jewish Jesters: A Study in American Popular Comedy (Berger) 2
Johnson, Mark 17–19
Jokes and Their Relation to the Unconscious (Freud) 8; punchlines 23; syntagmatic structure 23; techniques found in jokes 24
"Jokes as text types" 22
Journal of Consumer Research 12
Journal of Humor Research 28

Kan, Christina 11
Kant, Immanuel 5, 7
Keaton, Buster 37
Krapp's Last Tape (Beckett) 40
Krazy Kat (Herriman) 52

Lakoff, George 17–19
Lesser, Simon 69
Leviathan 6
Lévi-Strauss, Claude 3, 15, 27, 85
Li'l Abner: A Study in American Satire (Berger) 1, 55
Li'l Abner comic strip (Capp) 1

Marx, Groucho 2
Marx, Karl 15
Mason, Jackie 2
Master and the Margarita (Bulgakov) 43
McGraw, A. Peter 11
Metaphors We Live By (Lakoff and Johnson) 17, 19
A Midsummer Night's Dream (Shakespeare) 69
Miles Gloriosus (Plautus) 2
Moliere, Jean Baptiste 5
Morphology of the Folktale (Propp) 3; Propp's functions (table) 25; syntagmatic structure of folktales 24–25

Nilsen, Don L.F. 28
Nixon, Richard 49

Norton Shakespeare Comedies (3rd edition) 87

paradigmatic analysis of texts: Alan Dundes on 27; binary oppositions in 27
Paton, George E. 7
Peirce, Charles Sanders 15, 21
performance in comedies: body language 60; facial expression 60; makeup and props 60; noises and sound effects 60; scenery 60; voice usage 60
Piddington, Ralph 7
"The Position of Humor in Human Communication" 10
Postmortem for a Postmodernist (Berger) 2
Powell, Chris 7
Propp, Vladimir 3, 24–26

Rabelais and His World (Bakhtin) 88
Rank, Otto 69

Saussure, Ferdinand de 15, 19, 21, 86
School for Scandal (Sheridan) 2, 34
Schopenhauer, Arthur 7
Scott, Andrew 68
Seinfeld, Jerry 2
"Semiotics of Humor" 14
Semiotics: The Basics (Chandler) 20
Shakespeare, William 3, 5, 26, 30, 68, 73, 80, 87, 89, 90
Shaw, George Bernard 52
Sheridan, Richard 34, 37
Simon, Neil 39
Sleepers (Allen) 45
Stewart, Jimmy 49
Stoppard, Tom 47
Sweet Madness (Fry) 9

Travesties (Stoppard) 47
Tucker, Harry 64
TV-Guided American (Berger) 1
Twain, Mark 5
Twelfth Night (Shakespeare) 2, 46

Volpone (Jonson) 45

Warren, Caleb 11
Wayne, John 49
Wilde, Oscar 53, 54

Youngman, Henny 2

Zillmann, D. 10, 11

www.ingramcontent.com/pod-product-compliance
Lightning Source LLC
Chambersburg PA
CBHW030142170426
43199CB00008B/176